AMERICAN
BALLADS AND SONGS

AMERICAN
BALLADS AND SONGS

COLLECTED AND EDITED BY
LOUISE POUND
PROFESSOR OF THE ENGLISH LANGUAGE
UNIVERSITY OF NEBRASKA

CHARLES SCRIBNER'S SONS   NEW YORK

TO
H. M. BELDEN

FOREWORD

When Louise Pound's *American Ballads and Songs* was first published in 1922 as part of its Modern Student's Library series by Charles Scribner's Sons, it was a unique and important book. D. K. Wilgus, historian of American folksong scholarship, points to it as "clearly a forerunner" of the academic folklore collections to follow from university presses in the 1920s and 1930s.[1] Earlier, in the latter part of the previous century and in the opening decades of this one, academic presentation of folksong collectanea was to be found mainly in the pages of *The Journal of American Folklore*. Prior to 1922, however, separate publication in book format consisted only of folksong check lists[2] or of purely regional[3] or specialist collections.[4] *American Ballads and*

[1] D. K. Wilgus, *Anglo-American Folksong Scholarship Since 1898* (New Brunswick, N.J., 1959), 191.

[2] H. M. Belden, *A Partial List of Song-Ballads and other Popular Poetry Known in Missouri* (Columbia, Mo., 1907; with additions, 1910); H. G. Shearin and J. H. Combs, *A Syllabus of Kentucky Folk-Songs* (Lexington, Ky., 1911); Louise Pound, *Folk-Song of Nebraska and the Central West* (Lincoln, Neb., 1914).

[3] Loraine Wyman and Howard Brockway, *Lonesome Tunes: Folk Songs from the Kentucky Mountains* (New York, 1916); Josephine McGill, *Folk-Songs of the Kentucky Mountains* (New York, London, 1917); Olive Dame Campbell and Cecil J. Sharp, *English Folk Songs from the Southern Appalachians* (New York, London, 1917); Edith B. Sturgis and Robert Hughes, *Songs from the Hills of Vermont* (New York, 1919); Henry W. Shoemaker, *North Pennsylvania Minstrelsy* (Altoona, Pa., 1919); Loraine Wyman and Howard Brockway, *Twenty Kentucky Mountain Songs* (Boston, 1920).

[4] N. Howard Thorp, *Songs of the Cowboys* (Estancia, N. M., 1908; enlarged edition, Boston, New York, 1921); John A. Lomax, *Cowboy Songs and Other Frontier Ballads* (New York, 1910; new edition, 1916); John A. Lomax, *Songs of the Cattle Trail and Cow Camp* (New York, 1919).

Songs was a "first" on at least two counts: (1) it set a model for organization, presenting its song texts in sections beginning with "English and Scottish Ballads in America" (the Child ballads), followed by "Other Imported Ballads and Songs" and "Native Ballads and Songs," and closing with several smaller miscellaneous sections; and (2) true to its title, it was the first *American* anthology, containing selections not only from Pound's Nebraska collection but including songs and ballads from other sections of the United States and even a few texts from Canada.

The ballads and songs in Dr. Pound's anthology were selected for the purpose of illustrating "the main classes and types [of traditional song] having currency in English-speaking North America" (p. xiii). Only Afro-American and Amer-Indian selections and children's songs were excluded as constituting separate subjects and deserving treatment in anthologies of their own (pp. xx, xxxviii). But this little volume contains more than just an excellent representation of the kinds of folksongs to be found in America—its Introduction is a storehouse of generally sound information on folksongs and ballads and their occurrence and dissemination. A few examples will illustrate this point.

Early in her Introduction (pp. xviii–xix), Dr. Pound cites her criteria for identifying traditional songs: oral transmission, variation, circulation through "a fair period of time," and the loss of "all sense of their authorship and origin" by their singers. Most American folksong collectors would find little to cavil at with these tests. What is perhaps amazing is that these tests have not been subjected to any great amount of criticism in the half century since she first stated them. It is also to her credit that, although a teacher of English language and literature, she refrained from imposing any ethnocentric esthetic criteria for determining the

characteristics of folksong and in selecting the ballads
and songs included in this anthology. Not that she
was incapable of making such judgments (see, for example, her comments on page xix concerning her in-
clusion in this book of "inferior pieces"), but rather
that she deferred to the singers' tastes and what appealed to their "folk consciousness." I think she might
even have given her approval to the new directions in
folklore scholarship emphasizing ethnoesthetics and the
native criticism of verbal arts.

Her comments on oicotypification (the accommoda-
tion of alien pieces to regional modes and characteristics
[p. xxi]); her distinction between "poetry of folk and
poetry of culture" (p. xxi); her refusal to review folksong
as a nearly dead tradition (pp. xxiii, xxxii); her recognition of the importance of the tune to the text, that
"the two are not to be separated" (pp. xxxii–xxxiii),
despite her omission of any melodies in this volume;
her short survey of the work done in collecting and publishing American folksongs precedent to her *American
Ballads and Songs* (pp. xxxvi–xxxviii)—for all of these
and for sharing her great knowledge with us in the pages
of the Introduction we must be grateful to Louise Pound.

On at least one more score we are in her debt. Her
statement on the importance of professional entertainers and of mass communication media in the circulation of songs is a clearer statement than that of any
who came before her and of most who follow after.
Though insisting on the essentially oral nature of traditional song, she is no cultural romantic demanding a
slavish belief in the *exclusive* orality of folksong transmission. She recognizes the importance of broadsides,
popular songsters, sheet music, newspapers, and phonographs in circulating old songs and introducing new
songs into the repertoires of singers. She points, too,
to the role in this process played by singers in traveling

troupes, medicine shows, circuses, plays, vaudeville programs, camp meetings, and temperance gatherings (pp.
xxx–xxxii). They may serve as potential and actual
sources for folksingers, but the songs do not become
folksongs until they have been absorbed into a stream
of oral performances separate from those sources.

We would be doing Dr. Pound and later American
folksong scholars a grave injustice if we were to leave
you with the idea that everything she said was gospel
truth or that there were no errors in her Introduction.
The faults, however, are far fewer than the strengths.
Two examples should suffice. Her statement that
"variations of the folk are instinctive and unconscious,
not deliberate" (p. xx) cannot go unchallenged. Though
a large number of the changes in folksong may be the
product of essentially unconscious processes such as
forgetting, faulty hearing, and misunderstanding, the
creative process is certainly a conscious act. Senti-
mentalization, local adaptation, and bowdlerization, for
example, are variation-producing processes of an overtly
conscious type.[5]

One must also take exception to Pound's unqualified
statement, "the more isolated the region, the better the
chance for the survival of old songs" (p. xxii). Though
relative isolation may account in part for the vitality of
folk traditions in some regions, MacEdward Leach's
field work in Labrador showed rather conclusively that
when not accompanied by a creative force through
which new songs can be introduced into a community,
isolation will, in fact, contribute to the decay and perhaps eventual demise of the tradition.[6]

But these are relatively minor criticisms. In the

---

[5]Tom Burns, "A Model for Textual Variation in Folksong,"
Folklore Forum III (1970), 49-56.
[6]MacEdward Leach, *Folk Ballads and Songs of the Lower Labrador
Coast* (Ottawa, 1965), 12.

final analysis one can complain only that the Introduction suffers somewhat from being wordy and repetitious. It covers all the bases, however, and there is considerably less fault to be found with what it says than with how it is said.

Before ending this Foreword, a short biographical note about the collector and editor of this little volume seems appropriate. Louise Pound (1872–1958) received her B.A. and M.A. degrees in her home town of Lincoln at the University of Nebraska, before obtaining her Ph.D at the University of Heidelberg in 1900. Beginning as a teaching fellow in English Literature at Nebraska in 1894, she worked her way through the ranks, becoming a full professor in 1912. She served in that capacity for thirty-three years before retiring in 1945, ending a teaching career that spanned more than half a century. She was the author of numerous articles on literature and language, but it was in the field of folklore that she made her strongest mark. Taking on most of her contemporaries, she was one of the leading antagonists in the ballad war waged over the theory of the communal creation of folksong. Between 1913 and 1921, her vitriolic pen made numerous attacks on its supporters until she virtually swept the field of them with the publication of her book-length refutation, *Poetic Origins and the Ballad* (1921).[7] Her other books include *American Ballads and Songs* (1922), reprinted here on the fiftieth anniversary of its original publication, *Selected Writings of Louise Pound* (1949), and *Nebraska Folklore*, earlier writings edited by Dr. Pound in 1957–58 but published posthumously in 1959. She held major offices in a large number of academic socie-

---

[7]For an excellent discussion of the ballad war over the communal theory, and of the part played in it by Louise Pound, see D. K. Wilgus, *Anglo-American Folksong Scholarship Since 1898* (New Brunswick, N.J., 1959), Chapters 1 and 2.

ties including American Dialect Society (president 1938–41), National Council of English Teachers (director 1915–19), and the American Folklore Society (president 1925–27). One of her greatest triumphs came only a few years before her death when she was elected the first woman president of the Modern Language Association (1954–55) at the age of eighty-two.

Kenneth S. Goldstein

Graduate Folklore and Folklife Department
University of Pennsylvania

PREFACE

This anthology is intended to present to lovers of traditional song such selections as shall illustrate the main classes and types having currency in English-speaking North America. The interest attaching to them is partly literary, partly historical, and partly the interest of folk-lore.

The choice of pieces has not been made on the ground of poetical quality, although this has been taken into account. The aim is rather to display the typical songs and ballads liked by the people and lingering among them. The arrangement is neither chronological nor regional but is based upon type of material. Some of the texts are printed for the first time while others have appeared in various places. Occasionally variant texts have been introduced, to illustrate the multiple forms which may be assumed by a single ballad. In a few instances, where it seemed to have interest, a manuscript version is reproduced *literatim*. The provenience of the ballad included is entered in the notes, and—where this can be determined—the history of the ballad is sketched. But an effort has been made not to burden the notes with great detail or abundant comment, since the purpose of the anthology is literary and illustrative rather than scholarly and critical.

The collection is addressed to students of poetry and lovers of folk-song and to those who care for traditional pieces as social documents which reflect the life and traditions of those who preserve them.

The editor wishes to make grateful acknowledg-
ment to Professors H. M. Belden, Lowry C. Wimberly,
Edwin F. Piper, Reed Smith and others, who have
assisted her in various ways, especially by sending her
desirable texts. Thanks are due to the Macmillan
Publishing Company for permission to reprint four or
five texts from the *Cowboy Songs* of John A. Lomax,
to the H. W. Gray Company for permission to print
a text from Miss Loraine Wyman and Howard Brockway's *Lonesome Tunes*, to Boosey and Company for
two texts from Miss Josephine McGill's *Folk Songs
of the Kentucky Mountains*, to the Princeton University
Press for a text from W. Roy Mackenzie's *The Quest of
the Ballad*, and to G. P. Putnam's Sons for the reprinting
of several texts from Mrs. Campbell's and Cecil J.
Sharp's *English Folk Songs from the Southern Appalachians*. The editor is indebted for the suggestion
that she make an anthology of American folk-song to
Mr. Carl Van Doren.

LOUISE POUND.

University of Nebraska.

CONTENTS

INTRODUCTION

I. The pieces in the following collection depend for their vitality upon oral, not upon written, transmission. They have a subliterate existence, as apart from verse preserved in a form fixed by the printed page. They are to be distinguished from folk-songs like *Yankee Doodle, John Brown, Hail Columbia*, although these well-known songs belong even more properly to the "people as a whole" than do the songs in this anthology. Those included here are known to singers in scattered places; they have circulation in certain regions, among certain groups; and some of them find very large currency indeed. But other regions of America and other classes of people do not know them at all. Patriotic songs like *America*, and those named above, have nation-wide popularity. They are the property, not of the folk in certain sections and groups, but of the people of the United States. Their currency is not sporadic but universal. The real distinction, however, between folk-songs of the one type and of the other does not hinge upon their degree of currency among the people; it is something quite different. Songs handed on by the printed page are static; traditional pieces, handed on orally from mouth to mouth, are in a state of flux. This is the most valid distinction which can be made for folk-song proper as differentiated from book or semi-literary verse or from popular song in general. Traditional songs, or genuine oral songs or folk-songs, have no existence fixed by print. They have no standard form but are continually changing.

Other characteristics of genuine folk-songs are that they have retained their vitality through a fair period of time and that all sense of their authorship and provenience has been lost by their singers. Criteria of *origin* for the genuineness of folk-song have no dependability. A body of folk-song is increased by pieces of many origins; especially by the adaptation of old pieces, and by the absorption and metamorphosis into the stream of oral tradition of popular verse of many book or literary types. The only valid tests of genuine folk-song are not based on manner of origin but are the three just named. Genuine folk-songs are not static but are in a state of flux; they have been handed down through a fair period of time; and all sense of their authorship and origin has been lost.

The songs included in the following volume are for the most part simple in type, and they have been gathered in many parts of the United States. They come from scattered sources and from the tongues of many kinds of singers. Both songs telling a story, or ballads proper, and purely lyrical pieces have been included. The dividing line is sometimes hard to draw; for ballads often lose their thread of story and become pure lyrics. The reverse process, namely, that songs in oral tradition gradually assume a narrative element and become ballads, appears rarely if at all. Inferior pieces are included liberally in the volume as well as those of better quality. Whatever types have appealed to the folk-consciousness sufficiently to win preservation for themselves have been held to deserve representation.

Some delimitations have been observed, however. Songs of the following types are well known to many singers who have never seen them in print, but they have not been given representation in these pages: patriotic pieces, like *America, Yankee Doodle,* or national songs like *John Brown, A Hot Time;* popular religious songs, like *Onward Christian Soldiers;* pseudo-negro songs, like *Sewanee River, My Old Kentucky Home;* sentimental songs, like *Juanita, Lorena, My Bonnie Lies Over the Ocean.* For one thing, such songs are very familiar. They are easily accessible in print and there are no fascinating mysteries connected with their history. But of more importance is the fact that they have not been dependent upon oral tradition for their perpetuation. Further, little representation is given in these pages to children's songs and game songs and nursery rhymes. These form a separate subject; and so, for the most part, do negro and pseudo-negro songs. The most genuine American oral literature of all, that of the American Indian, assuredly forms a separate and wholly distinct subject. It needs treatment by itself. It bulks large and is part of the social history of America; but it has been without influence on the native traditional song in the English tongue.

II. The oral versions of folk-song are practically innumerable. A book of the size of the present volume could be filled by the variant versions of half a dozen of the pieces included in it. But it should be borne in mind that the variations of the folk are instinctive and unconscious, not deliberate. There are countless shiftings and omissions or additions in the mouths of varying singers, but they are unintentional. Alteration arises through slips of memory, local adaptations (as the substitution of names), and through the omissions and the insertions of individual singers. Many are due to confusion with other ballads or to personal tastes or prejudices. Nor is it always the fortunate changes which persist, though some scholars seem to think this. Stupid or garrulous changes

persist also. Crossings with other ballads may disorder
a song until it remains merely a heap of confused mate-
rials. Another song may glide onward from generation to generation keeping the situation—generally a
tragic situation—which is its soul; but transforming
its phrases and stanzas. Sometimes very old narratives, despite their multiform transformations, have
in most variants not yet lost their thread of story
or become transformed beyond recognition. This
is the case in the well-known ballads *Lord Randal*[1] and
The Two Sisters.[2]

On the whole, the influence of folk-transmission is a
levelling influence. It conventionalizes according to
its traditions. The total effect of its alterations, con-
tributions, and curtailments is to bring homogeneity
in style and manner of narration. Imported songs,
once of totally different character, accommodate
themselves to the regional modes and characteristics
of their new home. Some effective incident or story,
presented in a simple memorable way, commends
itself to the folk-consciousness. Gradually it trans-
forms itself in agreement with the tastes and traditions
of the localities where it becomes domesticated, and
sometimes it ends as something quite different from
what it was when it began.

It is usual to look upon ballads with some degree of
indulgence as verse of a singularly "artless" kind.
For that reason those who are in reaction from book
verse find in it peculiar pleasure. The truth is, however, that the antithesis should be drawn between
poetry of the folk and poetry of culture, not poetry of
"art." Art is not the same thing as culture and is not
dependent upon it. The most primitive people may
have its own kind of art. Ballads are often themselves

---

[1] *Johnny Randall* (No. 1) in this collection.
[2] No. 4.

relics of culture poetry, and they have their own art, traditions, and etiquette. These may be naïve, but it would never occur to the singers to wish for innovations, or for something more elaborate. From the art, traditions, and etiquette that it knows, the folk never wavers. Departure from them, within the limits of a period or place, is out of the question. It is always surprising that such variety may appear in the handling of stock material, yet so little inventiveness be exhibited, or novelty in technique.

III. Ballad singing was once a dignified means of entertaining a company. There was singing at social gatherings and at the games and dances of young folks, as well as on occasions of more impromptu character. Singing of this type is now much restricted, but it lingers in out-of-the-way places, as in the chimney nooks of farm houses, or by the stove in the cross-roads store. Ballad singing is not often to be heard from beggars and cripples, as once so typically in the Old World, nor on village greens; but casual knots of listeners may still be entertained by them in the cabin, in the cornfield, or by the creek. Occasionally they are heard in village parlors, or here and there in the drawing rooms of cities. Bits of picturesque old songs may sometimes be heard from children, who learned them from neighboring families or picked them up in the street. Ballads are most alive in the mountainous regions of the Southeast and on Western ranches. The more isolated the region, the better the chance for the survival of old songs. They may be sung to the fiddle or accordion, the mouth-harp, or occasionally to a cabinet organ. In the Cumberland mountains they are still sung to the banjo or to the "dulcimore," a three-stringed instrument plucked with the fingers, descending from Elizabethan days.

It is often a difficult matter to secure songs from the singers with good voices and retentive memories who know them best. Every collector has had experience with those whose modesty or perversity or fear of ridicule makes them unwilling to sing, for purposes of notation, the pieces in their repertory.

Even in the older and more isolated regions the influx of modern music has replaced traditional pieces by those in contemporary vogue. And the lessening of illiteracy has made remote communities less dependent for entertainment on what has been handed down. The prestige has diminished of singers with large repertories for whom, as for their audiences, the printed page means nothing. The broad-sheets containing older songs have been destroyed with the passing of the taste for them. In some communities, religious motives have lain behind the discarding of traditional pieces. They were thought to be "ungodly" by their singers. As time goes on, the popularity of the vicarious music of the phonograph (with the possibilities of variety and novelty afforded by its records) and the introduction of other forms of amusement have lessened the amount of singing for entertainment. It is not to be expected that singing will die out. Probably there will always be circulation of older songs apart from the printed page, in outlying regions where growth and change come slowly; but traditional song will not play the same rôle as formerly, and the songs entering into oral currency will be fewer and shorter lived. At the present time, the very multiplicity of new pieces lessens the chance that many will survive. When rural folk were thrown back almost solely upon song for diversion, it loomed larger and was more likely to retain vitality.

As regards regional distribution, traditional songs of the character of those included in this volume are found

most abundantly in New England and in the Southern
Appalachian region, in the Southwest, and in the
Middle West. At least these are the regions which
have been canvassed with the best results by collectors.
Canada also has yielded material. Nearly any kind of
piece may be found in any region; but, on the whole,
English and Scottish pieces of the romantic and legendary type have been best preserved in New England
and in the South. As they have roamed westward
they have lost their archaic flavor and many of their
distinguishing touches. Pieces of all types which
have reached the West, even when ultimately from the
Old World, have lost their former associations, and
are likely to sound as though they sprang up in the
locality which preserves them.

IV. The characters and manners of the American
ballads betray their varying origins and the divergent
social groups among which they have lingered. In
the imported romantic and legendary ballads high-
born personages sometimes retain their titles of nobility
and their aristocratic adventures are not lost. More
often, if such pieces have been long in the New
World, the characters, localities, and stories are accom-
modated to a New World setting. There is loss of
romantic features and disappearance of many archaic
literary touches in expression. Manners remain ele-
mental. The preservation of the bare stories gives no
chance for explanation or for subtleties. Evil stands
out stark and goodness is equally unqualified. The
"true love" is simple and devoted, the parents stern
or harsh; lovers are eternally attached, or faithless
and murderous. Favorite characters in the imported
pieces are knights and ladies, apprentices from London,
lovers back from wars, highwaymen, criminals, and
thieves. On the whole, the Western songs are those

which reflect most faithfully local conditions and characters. They tell of privations on government claims, of mining fevers, of cattle and "bosses" and the adventures of cowboys, of shooting affrays, and of the confessions of criminals and rovers. The occasional theme of death for love, appearing in American ballads, reflects the survival in folk-literature of what was once a widespread literary convention. In the "complaints" of the troubadours and of their lyric successors, as the sonneteers, death from love was the inevitable prospect held out as in store for himself by the singer or the poet, if the object of his adoration did not prove kind. Verse of this type lasted into the sixteenth and seventeenth centuries. Dying for love is the theme of *Barbara Allen's Cruelty*, and it helps to fix the period from which this ballad must have emerged. But death from love as a central motive has passed from present-day song as it did long ago from book verse; though sentimental song in general plays as large a rôle as ever in popular literature. So has the murderous lover, who was once so conspicuous a figure, passed from contemporary verse, though he lingers in folk-song. There is little violence in song of the present day and there are fewer striking stories. Serious or tragic stories hardly play any part in the song of our own time. Nor is it probable that much popular contemporary song will win foothold or prove to be long-lived. A favorite like *Tipperary* will not persist as did *Willie Reilly*, for example, which has a clear-cut and popular story and which gained its currency through coming into use as a campaign song. In general, themes and modes which have long been given up in the circles that knew them first remain alive in out-of-the-way places. Folk literature reflects the tastes in themes, the characters, manners, and stories of book or semi-literary verse of earlier generations. A considerable section of it carries into the present the wreckage of the culture poetry of the past.

V. The type of traditional songs first to claim the interest and attention of American lovers of balladry is imported, namely, English and Scottish popular ballads surviving in the United States. Something of Old World legend and romance is echoed in these immigrants from the British Isles which have found a home in a new land. Next in interest comes the group of American songs which is in strongest contrast, namely, frontier, pioneer, or cowboy pieces: songs of emigrants westward, of frontier conditions, and frontier characters, or of outlaws and criminals and rovers. Both varieties of song, the imported and the Western, are shrinking in bulk, the one with the fading of such song at its Old World sources, hence in its importation by immigrants, the other with the advance of population into Western outposts. A third important group of American traditional songs consists of love pieces of various kinds, which, whether inherited or indigenous, mostly conform to Old World patterns. Such are songs of the constant or the inconstant lover, of the reunion of parted lovers, of the murderous lover, or of lovers thwarted. The forsaken girl is the theme of many ballads and songs, and many pieces hinge upon the attitude of harsh parents. Such songs are familiar and abundant on both sides of the Atlantic, and they need little illustration. Beside songs from older and from later British sources there are many which show derivation from, or reference to, Ireland. There are some American pieces which retain supernatural elements, or make allusion to the supernatural; but on the whole ballads of the supernatural play a shrunken rôle in the New World.

A rough classification of the remaining types of American song would include a few songs of shipwreck or of the lost at sea, some Indian or pseudo-Indian songs like *The Pretty Mohea* or *The Aged Indian*, many humorous songs or song-stories—often finding their chief hold upon the memory in some single line—like *I Wish I was Single Again* or *I'll Not Marry at All*, songs of highwaymen like the British Dick Turpin, the Australian Jack Donahoo, the American Jesse James, or of the pirate Captain Kidd. There are also many death-bed confession pieces and somewhat ephemeral songs of local murders, assassinations, and disasters. There are moralities and religious songs, temperance songs, pathetic songs of orphans and infants, songs of occupational pursuits like farm and ranch life and railway songs; and, lastly, traditional game and dance and nursery songs of American children. These last need a volume to themselves and have been given little space in these pages.

The colonists who came to this country from England in the seventeenth century undoubtedly brought with them folk-songs of many types then popular in England. The ungodly songs censored by Cotton Mather were probably street songs, amatory or ribald, which he wished to see replaced by those of more pious character. Among them may have been some of the traditional English and Scottish ballads. It is quite possible that a few Old World ballads have been recovered in this country in an earlier form than that which survives in England. This may be true for *Barbara Allen's Cruelty*, some texts of which—as pointed out by Professor C. Alphonso Smith[1]—supply a hiatus in the narrative of British texts; and it may be true for *The Maid Freed from the Gallows*. The song of *Betsy Brown*, when Professor Firth's text[2] is compared with

---

[1] "Ballads Surviving in the United States," *The Musical Quarterly*, January, 1916.

[2] *An American Garland* (1915), p. 69.

some of those found in this country, seems to have retained integrity better in its New World form. *The Romish Lady*, dating from the era of Protestant martyrs, remains very close in its American derivatives to the broadside text of the time of Charles II, which is the earliest text of it preserved in England. It seems to play little or no rôle in later British traditional song but has found a good deal of currency on this side of the Atlantic. Since colonial times, folk-songs have been brought over by nearly every influx of newcomers. Immigrants from Ireland especially have brought over many songs. One "classic" from this source, much adapted and disguised, is *The Dying Cowboy*.

Nothing indigenous lives from colonial times, so far as is known. Nor does anything live from the Revolutionary War and the days following, except *Yankee Doodle*, which is sung to an Irish melody, and a few patriotic songs. These have an established popularity quite apart from the traditional and the oral. They have entered into traditional currency but are far from dependent on it. A still recognizable indigenous piece from the eighteenth century is *Springfield Mountain*, which has had astonishing vitality in view of its inferior quality. From the War of 1812 remain a few fragments like the children's game song "We're Marching on to Old Quebec" and a song concerning the British ship, the Boxer. The Civil War left us *John Brown, Tramp, Tramp, Tramp, Marching through Georgia*, etc., but these, like *America* and *Hail, Columbia*, though they are usually called "American folk-songs," are not dependent for perpetuation upon oral tradition. Some battle and campaign songs, songs of special events, and elegiac pieces have survived from the Civil War. A number have been salvaged in Missouri by Professor H. M. Belden, and in the Cumberland Mountains by Professor H. G. Shearin. But songs of this

type have little interest and fade early. Many sentimental songs from the middle decades of the nineteenth
century are still current, notably Mrs. Norton's
Juanita and H. D. L. Webster's *Lorena*. These are
favorite songs among ranchmen, cowboys, and others,
who are utterly unconscious of their provenience.
But the great legacy for American song from the period
of the Civil War is the legacy of negro song, plantation
songs, and the pseudo-negro songs of composers like
Stephen C. Foster, Henry C. Work, Will S. Hays.
Owing to their distinctive qualities and peculiar appeal,
a striking number of these pieces remain in popular
currency, and they constitute an attractive portion of
our song. Some of the comic negro songs, like *Jim
Crow, Zip Coon, Settin' on a Rail*, which are still alive
in traditional circulation, date from a period earlier
than the Civil War; but all types of negro songs gained
impetus during the war period and they owe to the
feeling and the interests which were bound up with it
much of their diffusion and persistence. The Cuban
War, later in the century, bequeathed *There'll Be a
Hot Time in the Old Town Tonight* to folk-song, and the
recent European war will probably leave its quota of
favorites, though it is yet too early to predict which of
them will find longest life.

VI. Traditional songs differ in their origin, history,
and the impetus for their diffusion. To some pieces
dates can be affixed and their development followed.
Others come from an uncertain past. They seem to
issue from nowhere in particular and to roam unac-
countably from region to region. The chances of time
have made it impossible to determine the year or the
locality of their emergence, or to be certain of their
original form. To most lovers of traditional verse,
however, the source of a song seems a negligible matter.

The problem of its origin is of little interest except to the specialist. The fact of popular transmission and the circumstance that generations of singers have contributed to its modification, curtailment, or expansion, lend it its attraction. It is always surprising to learn how soon the memory of the history and authorship of popular songs is lost.

For indigenous ballads, a few generalizations may safely be made. A percentage reflect real events; but in general there is little connection with history, or the connection is of slight importance. A few had their genesis in local happenings chronicled by local poets. Some, like the ballads of the Meeks murder examined by Professor H. M. Belden,[1] have found but little diffusion. Others, like *Springfield Mountain*, wandered far from their starting point. *Young Charlotte* seems to have been carried widely over the United States by the peregrinations of its author. As a general thing, local ballads, made by some local bard, or improvised by individual contributors, are the most ephemeral of all ballads. They rarely survive except in chance fragments.. A considerable proportion of the pieces current in American folk-song were floated by singers in traveling troupes, especially by the old-time "entertainers" and minstrel troupes of various types; or they were carried over the country, in later days, through the agency of plays into which they were introduced. Since Elizabethan times this has been a notable source of impetus. Fletcher's *Knight of the Burning Pestle* mentions many popular songs of the day. One is *Little Musgrave and Lady Barnard*, which is still alive in this country, whether or not it is in England, and another is *The Romish Lady*, which is also yet alive. The early popularity in London circles of

---

[1] "A Study in Contemporary Balladry," *The Mid-West Quarterly*, vol. I, pp. 162–172.

other songs now part of traditional folk-song is attested
by their incorporation into or mention in other dramas.
Certainly many American songs owe their circulation
to their introduction into plays (like *After the Ball*
which was taken about the country in Hoyt's farce
A Trip to Chinatown), or to their being taken through
many states by bands of wandering singers. Many
songs gained wide popularity through the agency of
colored minstrel troupes. *Johnny Sands* was floated
by itinerant bands like the Continental Vocalists and
the Hutchinson Family, in the earlier half of the
nineteenth century. *In the Baggage Coach Ahead* got
its currency by being thrown on a curtain, with colored
slides, in vaudeville programs.

There were, however, many other modes of diffusion
and helps to vitality. Important were the "popular
songsters," or small song books of various types, and
the "broadsides," in sheet music form or containing
the words alone, which were sold by itinerant vendors
of patent medicine, or peddlers, or at booths established
at fairs, or in the wake of circuses or of wandering
entertainers. Many songs learned from singers in
childhood at the schoolhouse linger in the memory
when those of newer acquisition have been forgotten.
Popular pieces of a religious or moralizing nature
gained circulation at the camp meetings of revivalists,
and many songs found their impetus at temperance
gatherings. Western songs were sometimes handed
on or launched at old settlers' picnics, or were sung at
social gatherings at farms or ranches, or at the "play
parties" and dances of young people. One of the most
important sources of preservation and one which has
afforded to collectors many of their best texts is the
manuscript book, handed on from generation to generation, into which songs have been transcribed from oral
and other sources. Some newspapers have conducted

columns in which "old favorites" are reprinted for readers, or texts are called for by those who have forgotten them, or the search is stimulated for the complete texts of songs recalled in fragments. Many scrap-books have been made and handed on into which clippings from newspapers of old favorites have been pasted. Most of these sources of circulation are now declining, and some of them are no longer existent. For that matter, the handing on of songs by oral tradition has become more and more curtailed. It is far from extinct, and it is not to be expected that it will ever completely die out from the human race; but with the spread of literacy, the increasing circulation of printed matter, the introduction of phonographs, and the removal of old-time isolation, through the agency of railroads, automobiles, and (in these days) of airplanes, the singing of traditional songs plays a lessened rôle.

American folk-song as a whole has been imported from the Old World. This is becoming less true, but it still holds. Folk-songs are still brought across the Atlantic by newcomers; and a large percentage of the most striking and persistent pieces current in America are derived from Old World originals, English, Scottish, or Irish. Many survive which were brought over long ago, or they enter in new form with some shipload of immigrants. Songs recently imported still win foothold and then wander from community to community.

VII. Sometimes collectors of ballads and folk-songs preserve the music to which the texts are sung, but more often the words only are recorded. The salvage of melodies is desirable; for folk-music, like folk-literature, has its interest and its distinctive ways. Generally the melody and the words are so associated in the minds of the singers that the one cannot be recalled without

the other. The song is the life of the words; the two
are not to be separated. Nevertheless the recording
of the tune along with the words is less important for
throwing light on the history of the song than might
be thought. The words have more stability than the
music. A piece retains its identity by its story, or its
situations, or its characters; not by its melody. For
example, innumerable varying airs have been recorded
for *Barbara Allen, Lord Randal, The Dying Cowboy,
Babes in the Woods*. It is often difficult or impossible
to determine which melody is nearest to the original.
Many texts of many kinds may be sung to one air,
and many different airs may be employed for one text.
There is even greater fluctuation on the musical than
on the textual side of folk-song. Indeed, here is a
prolific source of crossings in ballads, of amalgamations,
and of exchange of refrains. Pieces sung to a familiar
air may assume some of the associations of that air.
Possibly some of the older English ballads have been
preserved to us in comparative integrity because they
were chanted or recited rather than sung. Professor
Child suggests for some of the old English ballads that
they sound as though they were recited, and *The
Complaint of Scotland* (1549) testifies to the recital
rather than the singing of certain Robin Hood pieces.
But it is through singing that folk-songs are handed
down. In America at least, pieces do not seem to be
continued in tradition through recital or chanting.
They persist because they are sung. It is the music,
however it fluctuate, which keeps them alive.

VIII. The ballads of Old World collectors seem
often to have been touched by skilful hands. Sir
Walter Scott rests under the suspicion of having
enhanced the poetical quality and vigor of many pieces,
and so do other collectors, from Bishop Percy onward.
Nothing of the kind has been true in America. The

songs gathered by native collectors have been left as they were and American texts can be accepted without qualification. Taken as a whole, they testify that, though ballads may both gain and lose by transmission, the latter is the more usual process. It is a mistake to affirm that traditional preservation ensures improvement, though it may help for a time. It shortens a long or diffuse piece, drops out non-essentials, and preserves dramatic scenes, bits of dialogue, and the situation which is the soul of the story. Salient passages come to stand out, old introductions are lost, while the critical features of the narrative, the dialogue and the turning points, remain. The "nobler wild-flower sort of poetry" may have become such by virtue of the sifting hands through which it has passed, or by virtue of the selective processes of the folk-memory. But in the majority of cases a folk-song deteriorates in oral tradition, developing incompleteness, incoherence, and sometimes garrulous protraction. An instance in point is the ballad of *Springfield Mountain* which originated in the eighteenth century and has survived only in oral form. The process of folk-transmission has not evolved it into a good ballad or improved it. It had little poetical merit at the beginning and its twentieth century derivatives have not remedied the weaknesses of the original. Another instance is the fine old song of *Barbara Allen's Cruelty* which emerges from the seventeenth century. In many later forms it has wholly lost its dignity and appeal. Even those songs which have been improved by the processes of folk-transmission in the end fall themselves into decay.

As to stylistic characteristics, some American songs are rough, frank, spirited, others picturesque and pathetic. The diction tends to be rugged, the meter crude, the tone unsophisticated. Though sometimes highly colored by emotion, the language of American oral song is plain. Finery and elegance are lost if they were ever present. The folk-memory is intent on story and situation and it cares little for coherence or ornament. The conventional epithets of the Old World ballads do not appear in American ballads and, except when inherited, as in *Johnny Randall*, or *Edward*, or *The Cruel Brother*, the legacy motive and the sequence mannerism of the English and Scottish ballads are wanting. Common, however, is the "Come all ye" formula of invitation at the opening. This is characteristic of later British and Irish ballads, and has been domesticated in America from immigrant song

IX. Conscious interest in the traditional balladry of the people arose in England in the eighteenth century. In the latter half of that century the effort to recover and make public pieces of especial interest was made by many collectors. The impulse took on added momentum in the nineteenth century and has maintained itself, gaining rather than losing, into the twentieth. American enthusiasm for ballads came a hundred years later. The latter half of the nineteenth century brought the first important attempts to gather and preserve songs in traditional currency. The names of historic collectors for America are those of Professor Francis James Child (1825–1896) of Harvard, whose interest in English and Scottish ballads led to his preservation of many such pieces in their New World form, William Wells Newell (1839–1907), a founder of the American Folk-Lore Society and a collector of the games and songs of American children, and Professor G. L. Kittredge, upon whom fell the mantle of Professor Child at Harvard. Professor Kittredge has interested himself in all kinds of American traditional pieces, not only in English and Scottish ballads in America; and he has done much to stimulate collection and study in many parts of the country. Something in the way of preservation has also been contributed by historians, though the pieces having chief interest for historians are, from the nature of things, transient. They are likely to be of the political or chronicle type, rather than of general human interest.

On the whole, the wish to gather and preserve popular song may be viewed as accompanying or growing out of the trend toward democracy. It parallels for literary history the change taking place in the history of society in general. Since the eighteenth century the attention of political thinkers has descended through the various strata of society until the lowest strata are now in the foreground of interest. It has often been pointed out that contemporary historians endeavor to chronicle the common man as well as the hero. The lowly may now serve as central characters in fiction and drama which were once concerned solely with patricians. Similarly, the interest of literary historians and of students and readers has extended downward from the masterpiece till it embraces the humble and unrecorded literature of the folk.

Texts of oral literature in America have been available hitherto mostly in scattered places. Perhaps the widest ranging and completest available repository of such songs and ballads is Mrs. Campbell's and Cecil J. Sharp's *English Folk Songs from the Southern Appalachians* (1917). Tunes as well as texts are entered in this collection, and the same is true of the smaller *Folk Songs of the Kentucky Mountains* (1917) of Josephine McGill, and *Lonesome Tunes* by Loraine Wyman and Howard Brockway (1916). Western cowboy songs, both oral verse and book verse, were collected and published in two volumes by John A. Lomax, *Cowboy Songs* (1914) and *Songs of the Cow*

Camp and the Cattle Trail (1919). N. Howard Thorp's *Songs of the Cowboys*, with an introduction by Alice Corbin Henderson, appeared in 1921. W. Roy Mackenzie has printed a number of texts salvaged in Nova Scotia in *The Quest of the Ballad* (1919). Many interesting texts have been published in the *Journal of American Folk-Lore* by such scholars as G. L. Kittredge, H. M. Belden, Phillips Barry, E. C. Perrow, A. H. Tolman, and Arthur Beatty. The late Professor H. G Shearin listed and analyzed the folk-songs of the Cumberland region in Kentucky; Phillips Barry has done the same thing for the North Atlantic states, and H. M. Belden for Missouri. Professor C. Alphonso Smith, as archivist of the Virginia Folk-Lore Society, has done much to preserve the oral verse of Virginia, and Professor John H. Cox has collected the traditional verse of West Virginia. The game and nursery songs of American children constitute a part of oral literature in America. The pioneer collector and editor of them is W. W. Newell, whose *Games and Songs of American Children* (1883) is a credit to American scholarship. Of late years his work has been supplemented by the studies of others in various volumes of *The Journal of American Folk-Lore*. A few ballad texts have been preserved in articles in popular periodicals. The general subject of balladry in America has been treated in the present writer's chapter on "Oral Literature in America," published in the *Cambridge History of American Literature*, Volume IV (1921), and in several sections of her *Poetic Origins and the Ballad* (1921). Professor H. M. Belden has written of balladry in America and of the relation of balladry to folk-lore in inaugural addresses as president of the American Folk-Lore Society. And Mr. Phillips Barry has written upon many special subjects connected with American folk-song in the same periodical (*The Journal of American Folk-Lore*) which contains the addresses of Professor Belden.

X. Among the most characteristically American of our folk-songs are slave-songs, and plantation songs, and negro or pseude-negro songs, comic or pathetic. These constitute a separate subject and they deserve treatment in a separate anthology of Afro-American song. Besides these, as characteristically American in flavor, should come Western and frontier pieces, as *Starving to Death on a Government Claim*, or *The Dreary Black Hills*, and American humorous songs, like *Joe Bowers* or *Johnny Sands*. Apart from these two groups, most of our American traditional songs have upon them the stamp of the Old World and fall into Old World patterns. Prevailingly they are tragic pieces. Their "strong situations" keep them alive and they derive from or are parallel to British songs. Usually they have exaggerated plots and often they have exaggerated morals. There are confessions of murder, like *Young McFee*, and there are many confession and death-bed pieces in general. *The Butcher's Boy* is one of the most widely circulated oral ballads in the language. It is known from Nova Scotia to Texas. *The Boston Burglar* has equally wide currency. Both are serious pieces and both are of British adaptation. The murder ballad is a type which still springs up occasionally, like the ballads of the Meeks murder in Missouri chronicled by Professor H. M. Belden. Professor W. R. Mackenzie has recorded some murder ballads from Nova Scotia, and Professor H. G. Shearin found a number in the Cumberland mountains. But, like all ballads which chronicle local events, this type is likely to be short-lived. In general the gloomy themes, especially the songs of domestic crime, which pleased earlier centuries did not give the same pleasure

in the late nineteenth century, and they do not please
the earlier twentieth century. The sentimental songs
of the present do not show the elegiac or "complaint"
turn of the older songs but tend to be humorous or
happier. On the whole, the emotional pitch of American pieces is low, especially when they are placed in
comparison with their European analogues. This is true
both for earlier pieces and for songs of the present day.

It is of interest to trace the waves of popularity
which arise and fade for types of popular song as they
do for verse which is to be read. The types of leading
interest to be noted for the nineteenth century include
the slave songs, comic songs, and general negro songs
which were popularized by troupes of negro singers
and by the old-time "minstrel" troupes of whites.
There was a wave of temperance songs of which a few
pieces remain, like *Don't Go out Tonight, Dear Father,
The Drunkard's Lone Child, The Teetotallers are Coming.*
Ballads and songs of the drunkard, and especially of
the drunkard's child, once played a considerable rôle.
There were many campaign and camp songs of the
Civil War period, but they have nearly disappeared.
Still rememberable is the rise to popularity of "coon"
songs, one of which, *Ta-ra-ra-ra boom de ay,* found its
way into European circulation. "Coon" songs proved,
however, so slight in text and so indefinite in structure
that they retained little foothold in traditional song.
Nor are the succeeding "rag-time" songs or "jazz"
songs likely to leave much of a legacy. There is little
in their texts which is distinctive enough to lodge in the
memory. No clear-cut story holds them together, and
the taste to which they appeal is transitory. Some
contribution to folk-tradition should be made by the
songs which were universalized in the days of the
World War; but it is yet too early to predict which, if
any of them, will endure. A characteristic which

distinguishes the serious songs of our own day, in
contrast with those popular earlier, is their "glad"
note, their optimistic endeavor to look on the bright
side of things; this is evidenced by such songs as
Smile, Smile, Smile, or *Pack up Your Troubles in Your
Old Kit Bag.* There was a stronger military note in
the songs emerging from earlier American wars; and
the zest for fighting which was characteristic of the
songs of mediæval wars is somewhat conspicuously
wanting in the songs popularized by the war which
has passed.

When set over against Old-World texts brought
together by collectors, the American texts of the same
songs seem noticeable for their brevity. Possibly the
same curtailment might be apparent for British texts
of the present, when compared with their earlier coun-
terparts; but it is certain that existing American
variants show marked abridgment alongside the
versions current across the Atlantic. Even when an
immigrant piece has not been shortened as to the
number of its stanzas or lines, there is likely to be loss
in the details of narration. That there is no shrinkage
in length may be the result merely of garrulous protraction or repetition, arising as essential features are
lost. The American tendency toward brevity may
be viewed as the result of the decaying influence of
time and migration; or it may be looked upon as part
of the general trend toward shortening seen in the
drama, the essay, and prose fiction, as well as in verse
narratives. Neither twentieth century singers nor
twentieth century audiences have the patience and
the sustained interest which were characteristic of
days less hurried and eager for variety. When everything else has been shortened or is in the process of
shortening, it should not be surprising that folk-songs
have shortened too.

XI. The interest in floating pieces that linger from generation to generation in popular song is partly literary and partly sociological. They have no salient historic value but they convey clear impressions of a state of society. On the surface there is difference for different generations and for different regions, in song modes, types of plots, types of characters, and social views. Below the surface appears the same round of simpler feelings, jealousies, ambitions, disappointments, characteristic of human nature in all periods. Impressive stories or situations are set forth in simple types of verse. Occasionally the interest of the student of literature lies in flashes of poetic value or suggestions of wistful beauty. He comes upon passages of unexpected charm. More often it is the unconsciousness and frankness of the narrative, the total suppression of comment and of superfluous matter, that appeals to the reader, by virtue of the contrast which it affords with book verse. This frank unconscious note which is the chief source of their appeal belongs *par excellence* to the middle period of a ballad's history. Sometimes the earliest texts are complex, then simplification appears, dramatic situations are brought into the foreground, superfluous details are lopped off, and links drop from sight. Only the simpler and more impressive stanzas are preserved. Some instances in point are *Jemmy and Nancy (Pretty Nancy of Yarmouth)* and *The Babes in the Wood*. The original text of *Pretty Nancy*, with its references to "The Barbados Lady," is semi-literary and has as many as 288 lines. Its derivative from the Appalachian region telling of "the perbadus lady"[1] is on its way toward incoherent trash. Bishop Percy's text of *The Babes in the Wood*

---

[1] Campbell and Sharp, *English Folk Songs from the Southern Appalachians*, No. 53.

has twenty-two stanzas and shows completeness and literary finish. Most current versions of this song have no more than three or four stanzas. When ballads are in their decadence they sink to the fragmentary, vulgarized, garrulous, or inconsequent, or they die away in burlesque. The appeal has gone and the text is of interest chiefly as exhibiting the last stage of a process. But the frank unconscious note of popular song is not to be thought of as the especial property of mediæval peasant throngs or minstrels. It is recurrent for traditional songs of all ages and all regions. It may be found in many of the songs in the following pages as well as in the older ballads of England and Scotland.

ENGLISH AND SCOTTISH
BALLADS
IN AMERICA

1

(A) JOHNNY RANDALL

"Where was you last night, Johnny Randall, my son?
Where was you last night, my heart's loving one?"
"A-fishing, a-fowling; mother, make my bed soon,
For I'm sick at my heart, and I fain would lie down."

"What had you for breakfast, my own pretty boy?
What had you for breakfast, my heart's loving joy?"
"Fresh trout and slow poison; mother, make my bed
    soon,
For I'm sick at my heart, and I fain would lie down."

"What will you will your brother, my own pretty boy?
What will you will your brother, my heart's loving
    joy?"
"My horse and my saddle; mother, make my bed soon,
For I'm sick at my heart, and I fain would lie down."

"What will you will your sister, my own pretty boy?
What will you will your sister, my heart's loving joy?"
"My watch and my fiddle, mother make my bed soon,
For I'm sick at my heart, and I fain would lie down."

"What will you will your mother, my own pretty boy,
What will you will your mother, my heart's loving
    joy?"
"A twisted hemp rope, for to hang her up high;
Mother, make my bed easy till I lie down and die."

(B) JIMMY RANDOLPH

"What you will to your father, Jimmy Randolph my
     son?
What you will to your father, my oldest, dearest
     one?"
"My horses, my buggies, mother make my bed soon,
For I am sick-hearted, and I want to lie down."

"What you will to your brothers, Jimmy Randolph my
     son?
What you will to your brothers, my oldest dearest one?"
"My mules and my waggons, mother make my bed
     soon,
For I am sick-hearted, and I want to lie down."

"What you will to your sisters, Jimmy Randolph my
     son,
What you will to your sisters, my oldest dearest one?"
"My gold and my silver, mother make my bed soon,
For I am sick-hearted and I want to lie down."

2

(A) LORD LOVEL

Lord Lovel was standing at his castle gate,
     A-combing his milk-white steed,
When up stepped Lady Nancy Belle,
     A-wishing her lover good speed, speed, speed,
     A-wishing her lover good speed.

"Where are you going, Lord Lovel?" she said,
  "Where are you going?" said she.
"I'm going, my love," Lord Lovel replied.
  "New countries for to see, see, see,
  New countries for to see."

Lord Lovel was gone just a year and a day,
  New countries for to see,
When languishing thoughts came over his mind,
  Lady Nancy he must go see, see, see,
  Lady Nancy he must go see.

He mounted upon his milk-white steed,
  And rode to far London town.
And there he heard St. Patrick's bells,
  And the people came mourning, around, round,
    round,
  And the people came mourning around.

"O who hath died?" Lord Lovel said,
  "O who hath died?" said he.
"A lady hath died," a woman replied,
  "And they call her Lady Nancy, -cy, -cy,
  And they call her Lady Nancy."

He ordered her grave to be opened wide,
  Her shroud to be folded down,
And there he kissed her pale cold cheeks
  Till the tears came trinkling down, down, down,
  Till the tears came trinkling down.

Lady Nancy she died on Good Friday,
   Lord Lovel he died on the morrow;
Lady Nancy she died for pure true love,
   Lord Lovel he died for sorrow.

(B) LORD LOVER

"O where are you going, Lord Lover," said she,
   "O where are you going?" said she.
"I am going, my Lady Nancy Bell,
   Foreign countries for to see."

"How long will you be gone, Lord Lover?" said she,
   "How long will you be gone?" said she.
"A year or two or, the fartherest, three,
   Then return to my Lady Nancy."

He had not been gone but a year and a day,
   Foreign countries for to see,
Till wondering thoughts came over him,
   "Lady Nancy Bell I must go see."

He rode and he rode on his mule quite stay,
   Till he come to London town.
And there he heard St. Patrick's bells
   And the people all morning around.

"O what is the matter?" Lord Lover, said he,
   "O what is the matter?" said he.

"Lord, a lady is dead," an old lady said,
   "And her name was Lady Nancy."

He ordered her grave to be opened wide,
   Her shroud to be torn down,
And there he kissed her cold pale lips,
   Till the tears came trinkling down.

Lady Nancy was buried in the cold church ground.
   Lord Lover was buried close by her;
And out of her bosom there grew a rose,
   And out of Lord Lover's a briar.

They grew and they grew to the church steeple high,
   Till they could grow no higher.
And there they tied in a true lover's knot
   For all true lovers to admire.

3

(A)   BARBERY ALLEN

It was early in the month of May,
   The rosebuds they were swelling;
Little Jimmy Grooves on his deathbed lay
   For the love of Barbery Allen.

He sent his servant into the town
   Where she'd been lately dwelling,

Saying, "Bring to me those beautiful cheeks,
　　If her name be Barbery Allen."

So he arose and he left the room
　　Where she'd been lately dwelling,
Saying, "You've been called upon this eve,
　　If your name be Barbery Allen."

Then she arose and went to the room
　　Where Jimmy was a-lying,
And these were the words she seemed to say:
　　"Young man, I think you're dying."

"That's so, that's so, my love," said he,
　　"I'm in a low condition;
One kiss from you would comfort me
　　If your name be Barbery Allen."

"One kiss from me you'll never receive
　　Although you are a-dying";
And every tongue did seem to say
　　"Hard-hearted Barbery Allen."

"O don't you remember a long time ago,
　　Way down in yonder tavern,
Where you drank your health to the ladies all,
　　But you slighted Barbery Allen?"

"Yes, I remember a long time ago,
　　Way down in yonder tavern,

Where I drank my health to the ladies all;
But my love was to Barbery Allen."

She had not gone more than half a mile
Till she saw the corpse a-coming;
Saying, "Lay those corpse before my eyes
That I may look upon them."

The more she looked the more she wept,
Till she burst out a-crying;
And then she kissed those tear cold cheeks
That she refused when dying.

"O mamma, mamma, go make my bed,
Go make it long and narrow;
Little Jimmy Grooves has died of love,
And I will die of sorrow.

"O mamma, mamma, go make my bed,
Go make it long and narrow;
Little Jimmy Grooves has died today,
And I will die tomorrow."

Little Jimmy was buried in the new churchyard
And Barbery close beside him,
And out of his grave grew a red rose,
And out of hers a briar.

They grew and grew to the old church top
Till they both could grow no higher,
And they both were tied in a true-lover's knot,
The red rose and the briar.

(B) BARBARA ALLEN

Honor, Honor, is the town
    In which three maids were dwelling.
There is only one I call my own,
    Her name is Barbara Allen.

He sent his servant to her town
    And he sent him to her dwelling.
"My master, O he's very sick
    For the love of Barbara Allen."

Slowly, slowly she rose up,
    And to his bedside was going.
She pulled the curtains to aside
    And said "Young man, you're a-dying."

He stretched out his pale white hand,
    Expecting to touch hers,
She hopped and skipped all over the floor
    And "Young man, I won't have ye."

Sweet William died on Saturday night,
    And Barbara on Sunday.
The Old Woman died last of all,
    She died on Easter Monday.

4

(A) THE TWO SISTERS

"O sister, O sister, come go with me,
Go with me down to the sea."

> Jury flower gent the rose-berry,
> The jury hangs over the rose-berry.

She picked her up all in her strong arms
And threwed her sister into the sea.

"O sister, O sister, give me your glove,
And you may have my own true love."

"O sister, O sister, give me your hand,
And you may have my house and land."

"O sister, O sister, I'll not give you my hand,
And I will have your house and land."

O the farmer's wife was sitting on a rock.
Tying and a-sewing of a black silk knot.

"O farmer, O farmer, run here and see
What's this a-floating here by me."

"It's no fish and it's no swan,
For the water's drowned a gay lady."

The farmer run with his great hook
And hooked this fair lady out of the sea.

"O what will we do with her fingers so small?"
"We'll take them and we'll make harp screws."

"O what will we do with her hair so long?"
"We'll take it and we'll make harp strings."

O the farmer was hung by the gallows so high,
And the sister was burned at the stake close by.

(B)   THE OLD MAN IN THE NORTH COUNTREE

There was an old man in the North Countree,
  Bow down
There was an old man in the North Countree,
  And a bow 'twas unto me
There was an old man in the North Countree,
He had daughters one, two, three.
  I'll be true to my love if my love is true to me.

There was a young man came a-courting
And he made choice of the youngest one.

He gave his love a beaver cape;
The second she thought much of that.

"Sister, O sister, let us go down
And see the ships go sailing by."

As they was a-walking by the saucy brimside
The oldest pushed the youngest in.

"Sister, O sister lend me your hand, a
And I'll give you my house and land."

"What care I for house and lands?
All that I want is your true love's hand."

Down she sunk and away she swam
Till she came to the miller's mill-dam.

The miller ran out with his fish-hook
And fished the maiden out of the brook.

"The miller shall be hung on his own mill-gate
For drownding my poor sister Kate."

5

(A) THE JEWISH LADY

It rained a mist, it rained a mist,
  It rained all over the land;
Till all the boys throughout the town
  Went out to toss their ball, ball, ball,
  Went out to toss their ball.

At first they tossed their ball too high,
  And then again too low,

Till over in the Jewish garden it fell,
   Where no one was darst to go, go, go,
   Where no one was darst to go.

Out came a Jewish lady,
   All dressed so gay and fine.
"Come in, my pretty little boy," she said,
   "And you shall have your ball, ball, ball,
   And you shall have your ball."

At first she showed him a yellow apple dish,
   And a gay gold ring,
And then a cherry as red as blood,
   To entice this little boy in, in, in,
   To entice this little boy in.

She took him by his little white hand,
   And led him through the hall,
And then unto a cellar so deep,
   Where no one could hear him lament, lament,
   Where no one could hear him lament.

"If any of my playmates should call for me,
   You may tell them that I'm asleep;
But if my mother should call for me,
   You may tell her that I am dead,
And buried with a prayer-book at my feet,
   And a bible at my head, head, head,
   And a bible at my head."

(B) THE JEW LADY

My ball flew over in a Jew's garden,
  Where no one dared to go,
I saw a Jew lady in a green silk dress
  A-standing by the do'.

"Come in, come in, my pretty little boy,
  You may have your ball again."
"I won't, I won't, I won't come in,
  Because my heart is blood."

She took me then by her lily-white hand,
  And led me in the kitchen,
She sot me down on a golden chair,
  And fed me on sugar and rice.

She took me then by her lily-white hand,
  And led me in the kitchen,
She laid me down on a golden plank,
  And stobbed me like a sheep.

"You lay my Bible at my head,
  And my prayer book at my feet,
And if any of my playmates they ask for me,
  Just tell them I've gone to sleep."

6

(A) THE WIFE WRAPPED IN A WETHER'S SKIN

Sweet William married him a wife,
  Jennifer June and the Rosemaree
To be the sweet comfort of his life.
  As the dew flies over the green vallee.

It's she couldn't into the kitchen go,
For fear of soiling her white-heeled shoes.

It's she couldn't wash and she wouldn't bake,
For fear of soiling her white apron-tape.

It's she couldn't card and she wouldn't spin,
For fear of spoiling her delicate skin.

Sweet William came whistling in from the plow;
Says, "O my dear wife, is my dinner ready now?"

She called him a dirty paltry whelp:
"If you want any dinner, go get it yourself."

Sweet William went out unto the sheepfold,
And out a fat wether he did pull.

Upon his knees he did kneel down,
And soon from it did strip the skin.

He laid the skin on his wife's back
And he made the stick go whickety whack.

"I'll tell my father and all his kin
How you this quarrel did begin."

"You may tell your father and all your kin
How I have thrashed my fat wether's skin."

Sweet William came whistling in from the plow,
Says, "O my dear wife, is my dinner ready now?"

She drew her table and spread her board,
And 'twas "O my dear husband," with every word.

And now they live free from all care and strife,
And now she makes William a very good wife.

(B)   DANDOO

A little old man lived in the west,
   Dandoo, dandoo
A little old man lived in the west,
   Clamadore clash may clings
A little old man lived in the west,
He had a little wife that was none of the best.
   And a lambo scrambo churum churum
   Calla may clash may clings.

This little old man came in from his plow,
Saying, "Honey have you got my breakfast now?"

"There lays a piece of cold bread on the shelf.
If you want any more you can get it yourself."

He drew the old wether up to the pin,
And at three jerks fetched off his skin.

He threw the sheep's skin around his wife's back,
And two little sticks went whickety whack.

7

(A)   CHILDREN'S SONG

The starry light and the lady bright,
    Her children she had three.
She sent them away to the North country
    To learn those gramerie.

They hadn't been gone but a very short time,
    Scarce three months and a day,
Till death came rushing along over the land
    And swept those babes away.

Their mother came as far to know,
    She wrung her hands full sore.
"The less, the less, the less!" she cried,
    "Shall I see my babes no more?"

"There were a king in heaven," she said,
    "That used to wear a crown;

Send all my three little babes tonight
  Or in the morning soon."

Or Christmas times were drawing nigh,
  The nights were long and cold;
Her three little babes came rushing along
  Down to their mother's hall.

She fixed them a table in the dining room,
  Spread over with bread and wine;
Saying, "Eat, O, eat my sweet little babes;
  Come eat and drink of mine."

"Mama, we cannot eat your bread,
  Nor we can't drink your wine;
For yonder stands our Saviour dear,
  And to him we'll return."

She fixed them a bed in the backmost room,
  Spread over with a clean sheet,
And a golden wine upon the top of them
  To make them sweeter sleep.

"Take it off, take it off," says the oldest one,
  "The cocks they will soon crow;
For yonder stands our Saviour dear,
  And to him we must go.

"Cold clods lays on our feet, mama;
  Green grass grows over our heads;
The tears that run all down our cheeks
  Did wet the winding sheets."

(B)   THREE LITTLE BABES

Christmas time was drawing near
   And the nights were growing cold,
When three little babes came running down
   Into their mother's fold.

She spread a table long and wide,
   And on it put bread and wine.
"Come eat, come drink, my sweet little babes;
   Come eat and drink of mine."

"We want none of your bread, mother,
   We want none of your wine,
For yonder stands our blessed Lord
   And to Him we will join."

She made a bed in the very best room,
   And on it put clean sheets,
And over the top a golden spread,
   The sweeter they might sleep.

"Take it off, take it off," cried the eldest one,
   "Take it off," cried he,
"For I would not stay in this wicked world,
   Since Christ has died for me.

"A sad farewell, kind mother dear,
  We give the parting hand,
To meet again on that fair shore
  In Canaan's happy land.

"A tombstone at our head, mother,
  The cold clay at our feet;
The tears we have shed for you, mother,
  Have wet these winding sheets."

8

THE CRUEL BROTHER

Three ladies played at cup and ball,—
  With a hey! and my lily gay!
Three knights there came among them all.
  The rose it smells so sweetly.

And one of them was dressed in green,—
He asked me to be his queen.

And one of them was dressed in yellow,—
He asked me to be his fellow.

And one of them was dressed in red,—
He asked me with him to wed.

"But you must ask my father the King,
And you must ask my mother the Queen,—

"And you must ask my sister Anne,
And you must ask my brother John."

"O I have asked your father the King,
And I have asked your mother the Queen,—

"And I have asked your sister Anne,
And I have asked your brother John."

Her father led her down the stairs,
Her mother led her down the hall.

Her sister Anne led her down the walk,
Her brother John put her on her horse.

And as she stooped to give him a kiss,
He stuck a penknife into her breast.

"Ride up, ride up, my foremost man!
Methinks my lady looks pale and wan!"

"O what will you leave to your father the King?"
"The golden coach that I ride in."

"And what will you leave to your mother the
    Queen?"
"The golden chair that I sit in."

"And what will you leave to your sister Anne?"
"My silver brooch and golden fan."

"And what will you leave to your brother John?"
"A pair of gallows to hang him on."

"And what will you leave to your brother John's
      wife?"
"Grief and misfortune all her life."

9

EDWARD

"How come that blood on your shirt sleeve,
  Pray son, now tell to me?"
"It is the blood of the old greyhound,
  That run young fox for me."

"It is too pale for that old greyhound,
  Pray son, now tell to me."
"It is the blood of the old grey mare,
  That ploughed that corn for me."

"It is too pale for that old grey mare,
  Pray son, now tell to me."
"It is the blood of my youngest brother
  That hoed that corn for me."

"What did you fall out about,
  Pray son, now tell to me?"
' Because he cut yon holly bush
  Which might have made a tree."

"O what will you tell to your father dear,
   When he comes home from town?"
"I'll set my foot in yonder ship
   And sail the ocean round."

"O what will you do with your sweet little wife,
   Pray son, now tell to me?"
"I'll set her foot in yonder ship
   To keep me company."

"O what will you do with your three little babes,
   Pray son, now tell to me?"
"I'll leave them here, in the care of you,
   For to keep you company."

"O what will you do with your house and your land,
   Pray son, now tell to me?"
"I'll leave it here, in care of you,
   For to set my children free."

10

THE LOWLANDS LOW

Up then spake our noble cabin boy,
Saying, "What will you give me if I will them destroy?
If I will them destroy, send them floating o'er the tide,
And sink them in the Lowlands, the Lowlands low,
And sink them in the Lowlands low?"

"O the man that them destroys," the captain made
     reply,
"A fortune he shall have and my daughter to wife,
A fortune he shall have and my daughter beside,
If he'll sink them in the Lowlands, the Lowlands low,
If he'll sink them in the Lowlands low."

The one was playing at cards and the other playing at
     dice,
The boy swam up and he scuttled them so nice,
He scuttled them so nice, sent them floating with the
     tide,
And sank them in the Lowlands low,
And sank them in the Lowlands low.

The boy swam first unto the starboard side,
Saying, "Captain pick me up for I'm wearied with the
     tide,
O Captain pick me up for I'm wearied with the tide
And I'm sinking in the Lowlands, the Lowlands low,
And I'm sinking in the Lowlands low."

"O no," replied the Captain, "I will not pick you up,
I will sink you, I will shoot you, send you floating with
     the tide,
I will sink you, I will shoot you, send you floating with
     the tide,
And I'll sink you in the Lowlands, the Lowlands low,
And I'll sink you in the Lowlands low."

The boy swam round unto the larboard side,
Saying, "Messmates, pick me up, for I'm wearied with
the tide,
O messmates, pick me up for I'm wearied with the
tide.
And I'm sinking in the Lowlands, the Lowlands low,
And I'm sinking in the Lowlands low."

His messmates picked him up, and on the deck he died.
They sewed him up in his hammock so wide,
They sewed him up, sent him floating with the tide,
And they sank him in the Lowlands, the Lowlands low,
And they sank him in the Lowlands low.

11

THREE SAILOR BOYS

Up spoke the man of our gallant ship,
    And a well spoken man was he,
Saying, "I married me a wife in a far distant town,
    And tonight a widow she will be, be, be,
    And tonight a widow she will be."

> For the roaring sea, they do roar, O roar,
> And the stormy winds they do blow,
> As the three poor sailor boys they were mounted
>   up aloft,
> While the love land was lying down below, down
>   below,
> While the love land was lying down below.

Up spoke the boy of our gallant ship,
 And a well spoken boy was he,
Saying, "I have a true love in a far distant town,
 And tonight she'll be wailing for me, for me,
 And tonight she'll be wailing for me."

Up spoke the girl of our gallant ship,
 And a well spoken girl was she,
Saying, "I have been used to sleeping on a soft feather
  bed,
 And tonight on the bottom of the sea, the sea,
 And tonight on the bottom of the sea."

Up spoke the cook of our gallant ship,
 And a greasy old thing was she,
Saying, "I can have more fun with my kettles and my
  pots
 Than to sink to the bottom of the sea, the sea,
 Than to sink to the bottom of the sea."

Six times around sails our gallant ship,
 Six times around sails she,
Six times around sails our gallant ship,
 And she sank to the bottom of the sea, the sea,
 And she sank to the bottom of the sea.

12

LORD THOMAS

 Lord Thomas he was a bold forester,
  The chaser of the king's deer;

Fair Ellen she was a sweet young lady,
   Lord Thomas he loved her dear.

"Come riddle my riddle, dear mother," he said,
   "Come riddle it all in one,
Whether I shall marry fair Ellen or no
   Or bring the brown girl home."

"The brown girl she has houses and land,
   Fair Ellen she has none,
So I advise you with my blessing
   To bring the brown girl home."

Lord Thomas he dressed in scarlet red,
   His merry men all were seen,
And as he rode along the street,
   They took him to be a king.

He rode till he came to fair Ellen's gate,
   He knocked loud at the ring,
And who was there but fair Ellen herself
   To let Lord Thomas in?

"What news, what news?" fair Ellen said,
   "What news have you brought me?"
"I've come to invite you to my wedding,
   Most miserable news for thee."

"O God forbid," fair Ellen she said,
   "That such a thing should be done,

I thought to be the bride myself
   And thou shouldst be the groom."

"Come riddle my riddle, dear mother," she said,
   "Come riddle it all in one,
Whether I shall go to Lord Thomas' wedding,
   Or shall I stay at home?"

"O to Lord Thomas' wedding don't go,
   To Lord Thomas' wedding don't go;
As many as are your friends, dear daughter,
   There's more will be your foes."

"To Lord Thomas' wedding I'll go," she said,
   "To Lord Thomas' wedding I'll go,
If it costs my heart's blood, body and all,
   To Lord Thomas' wedding I'll go."

Fair Ellen she dressed in scarlet red,
   Her merry maids all were seen,
And as she rode along the street
   They took her to be a queen.

She rode till she came to Lord Thomas' gate,
   She knocked loud at the ring.
And who was there but Lord Thomas himself
   To let fair Ellen in.

He took her by her lily-white hand,
   He led her through the hall;

He placed her on the noblest chair
   Among the ladies all.

"Is this your bride?" fair Ellen said,
   "I think she is wonderful brown,
You might have had as fair a young lady
   As ever put foot on ground."

"Despise her not," Lord Thomas he said,
   "Despise her not unto me;
Better I love your little finger
   Than the brown girl's whole body."

The brown girl she had a little pen-knife,
   It was both keen and sharp;
Betwixt the long ribs and the short
   She pierced fair Ellen's heart.

"What ails, what ails?" Lord Thomas he said,
   "I think you are wonderful pale;
You used to have so fair a color,
   As ever a rose could bloom."

"O are you blind," fair Ellen said,
   "Or can you not very well see?
O don't you see my own heart's blood
   Go trickling down my knee?"

Lord Thomas he had a two-edged sword,
   He flourished it all around;

He took the brown girl's head from the shoulders
    And threw it to the ground.

He put the handle on the ground,
    The point was towards his heart.
Those three true lovers they very well met,
    But sadly they did depart.

"O dig my grave," Lord Thomas he said,
    "Dig it both wide and deep,
And lay fair Ellen in my arms,
    And the brown girl at my feet."

Out of Lord Thomas there grew a golden briar,
    And out of fair Ellen a thorn;
Those three true lovers they very well met,
    But better they'd never been born.

13

THE HANGMAN'S SONG

"Hangman, hangman, slack up your rope,
    O slack it for a while,
I looked over yonder and I see Paw coming,
    He's walked for many a long mile."

"Say Paw, say Paw, have you brung me any gold,
    Any gold for to pay my fine?"
"No sir, no sir, I've brung you no gold,

No gold for to pay your fine,
But I'm just come for to see you hanged,
Hanged on the gallows line."

"O you won't love and it's hard to be beloved
And it's hard to make up your time,
You have broke the heart of many a true love,
True love, but you won't break mine."

"Hangman, hangman, slack up your rope,
O slack it for a while,
I looked over yonder and I see Maw coming,
She's walked for many a long mile."

"Say Maw, say Maw, have you brought me any
gold,
Any gold for to pay my fine?"
"No sir, no sir, I've brought you no gold,
No gold for to pay your fine,
But I'm just come for to see you hanged,
Hanged on the gallows line."

"O you won't love and it's hard to be beloved,
And it's hard to make up your time,
You have broken the heart of many a true love,
True love, but you won't break mine."

    *   *   *   *   *   *

"Hangman, hangman, slack up your rope,
O slack it for a while,

I looked over yonder and I see my sweetheart
    coming,
  She's walked for many a long mile."

"Sweetheart, sweetheart, have you brought me
    any gold,
  Any gold for to pay my fine?"
"Yes sir, yes sir, I've brought you some gold,
  Some gold for to pay your fine,
For I'm just come for to take you home,
  From on the gallows line."

14

LORD BAYHAM

Lord Bayham was a brave young man,
  He was as brave as brave could be;
He grew oneasy and discontented
  Till he had taken a voyage to sea.

He was blown east, he was blown west,
  He was blown to some Turkish shore,
Where the Turks they got him and sorely used him;
  He vowed for freedom any more.

They bored a hole through his left shoulder,
  And bound him fast unto a tree,
And gave him nothing but bread and water,
  Bread and water once a day.

The Turks they had one only daughter,
    She was as fair as fair could be;
She stole the keys of her father's prison,
    And vowed Lord Bayham she would set free.

"O have you land, or have you living,
    Or have you houses, many, free,
That you could give to a Turkish lady
    If out of prison she'd set you free?"

"Yes, I have land and I have living,
    And I have houses, many free,
I'll give them all to you, pretty creature,
    If out of prison you'll set me free."

She led him down to her father's cellar,
    And drawed to him the best port wine,
And drank a health; those words did follow,
    "Lord Bayham, if you were but mine!"

O now the notes of love were drawn,
    And seven years they were to stand;
He was to marry no other woman,
    Unless she married some other man.

She led him down to the sea shore,
    And sat him sailing on the main.
"Farewell, farewell, my own dear jewel,
    When shall I see your fair face again!"

Seven years were gone and past,
  And seven weeks and almost three,
She bundled up her silks and rubies,
  And vowed Lord Bayham she would see.

And when she got to Lord Bayham's gate,
  She knocked so loud she made it ring.
"Who's there? Who's there?" cried the young
    proud porter,
  "That knocks so loud and won't come in."

"Is this Lord Bayham's land and living?
  Or is Lord Bayham himself at home?"
"This is Lord Bayham's land and living.
  He has this day fetched a young bride home."

"I've a gold ring on every finger,
  And on my middle finger three.
I'll give them all to you, young proud porter,
  If you will do one thing for me.   .   .   ."

"Go down into your father's cellar,
  And draw to me the best port wine,
And drink a health to a prince's daughter,
  Who freed you from your prison bound."

He went unto his master dear,
  And fell low down upon his knees.
"Rise up, rise up, you young proud porter,
  What news have you brought unto me?"

"This seven weeks I kept your gates,
   And seven weeks and almost three,
There's the fairest lady stands at your gates
   That ever my two eyes did see.

"She has a gold ring on every finger,
   And on the middle finger three;
She has more fine gold around her waist
   Than would buy old England, France, and thee."

Lord Bayham rose upon his feet,
   And split his table in pieces three,
Saying, "I'll forfeit all my land and living
   That the Turkish lady has crossed the sea."

Then up bespoke the young bride's mother,
   Those words in anger she did say;
"Would you forsake my own dear daughter,
   And marry a Turkish lady?"

He says, "Here is your daughter as I got her.
   I'm sure she is none the worse of me.
She came to me on a horse and saddle,
   I'll send her home in her coach and three."

He took Susan by her little white hands,
   And led her down the golden stream,
And changed her name from lovely Susan,
   And called her Lord Bayham's queen.

15

LITTLE MATTHY GROVES

The first come down was a raven white,
And the next come down was a polly,
And the next come down was Lord Thomas's wife,
And she was the fairest of them all, all,
And she was the fairest of them all.

Little Matthy Groves was a-standing by;
She placed her eyes on him,
Saying: "You're the darling of my heart
And the darling of my life.

"It's you no home, no place to lie,
Go home with me this night."
"I think by the rings you wear on your fingers
You are Lord Thomas's wife."

"True I am Lord Thomas's wife,
Lord Thomas is not at home."
The little foot-page was a-standing by,
These words heareth he,
And he licked to his heels and run.

He run, he run to the broken-down bridge,
He bent to his breast and swum;
He swum, he swum to the other, other side,
And he buckled up his shoes and he run.

He run, he run to Lord Thomas's gate,
And he dingled at the ring and it rung,
And he dingled at the ring and it rung.
"What news, what news, my little foot-page?
What news you've brought to me?"
"Little Matthy Groves is at your house
In bed with the gay lady."

"If that be a lie you've brought to me,
And a lie I expect it to be,
If there is e'er a green tree in these whole worlds,
A hangman you shall be.

"If that be the truth you've brought to me,
And the truth I don't expect it to be,
You may wed my youngest daughter,
And you may have all I've got."

Lord Thomas's wife raised up about half a doze asleep.
"Lay still, lay still," little Matthy Groves says,
"Lay still, I tell to thee,
For it's nothing but your father's little shepherd boy
A-driving the wolves from the sheep."

When little Matthy Groves did wake
Lord Thomas was at his feet.
"Rise up, rise up," Lord Thomas he says,
"And put your clothing on,
For it never shall be known in old England
That I slew a naked man.

"How can I rise up, "he says,
"When I am afeard of my life?
For you have two good broad-edged swords
And I have not so much as a knife."

"True I have two good broad swords,
They cost me deep in the purse.
But you may have the very best one,
And you may have the first lick."

The very first lick little Matthy Groves struck,
He struck him across the head,
And the very next lick Lord Thomas he struck,
And it killed little Matthy Groves dead.

He took his gay lady by the hand,
And he led her up and down.
He says: "How do you like my blankets
And how do you like my sheets?"

"Well enough your blankets,
And well enough your sheets,
But much better do I love little Matthy Groves
Within my arms asleep."

He took his gay lady by the hand,
And he pulled her on his knee,
And the very best sword that he did have
He split her head into twine.

16

SWEET WILLIAM

Sweet William arose on last May morning,
  And dressed himself in blue;
"Come tell unto me that long, long love
  Between Lyddy Margret and you."

"I know no haɪm of Lyddy Margret, my love,
  I'm sure she knows none of me;
By eight o'clock tomorrow morning
  Lyddy Margret my bride shall see."

Lyddy Margret was sitting in her own bower room
  A-combing her yellow hair;
She saw Sweet William and his new bride
  As they came riding near.

Lyddy Margret threw down her golden comb,
  And quickly she bound up her hair;
And away she went from her own bower room,
  No more to be seen there.

The day being past and night come on
  When all men were asleep,
Lyddy Margret's ghost came about midnight
  And stood at Sweet William's bed feet.

"How do you like your bed?" she said,
  "How do you like your sheet;

How do you like that fair ladie
  That lies in your arms asleep?"

"Very well I like my bed," he said,
  "Very well I like my sheet;
But better I like the fair ladie
  That stands at my bed feet."

The night being gone and day come on,
  When all men were awake;
Sweet William he rose with trouble on his mind
  From the dream that he dreamed last night.

"Such dreams, such dreams as I dreamed last night,
  Such dreams are never good;
I dreamed my room was full of wild swine,
  My bride bed full of blood."

Sweet William he called his merry men all
  By ones, by twos, by threes;
Before them all he asked his bride
  If Lyddy Margret he might go see.

"What will you do with Lyddy Margret, my love,
  And what will you do with me?"
"Today I go see Lyddy Margret," he said,
  "Tomorrow return to thee."

He rode till he came to Lyddy Margret's hall,
  And dingled so loud on the ring;

And who so ready as her own brothers
  To rise and let him come in?

"Is Margret in her own bower room,
  Or is she in her hall,
Or is she in the kitchen
  Among her merry maids all?"

"She's neither in the kitchen,
  She's neither in her hall;
But she is in her own bower room
  Laid out against the wall."

"Raise up, raise up that coffin lid
  So I can gaze within;
And let me kiss her clay-cold lips
  Lord send it the breath was in."

First he kissed her on the cheek,
  And then he kissed her chin;
And then he kissed her clay-cold lips
  That oft times had kissed him.

"Fold down, fold down those snowy white sheets,
  All made of linen so fine;
Today they hang over Margret's corpse,
  Tomorrow hang over mine."

Lyddy Margret died it might have been today,
  Sweet William died tomorrow.

Lyddy Margret died for pure, pure love,
  Sweet William died for sorrow.

Lyddy Margret was buried in the lower church yard,
  Sweet William was buried in the higher;
And out of her grave there sprang a red rose,
  And out of his grave a briar.

They grew and they grew to the high church top,
  And then they could grow no higher;
And there they tied in a true lover's knot
  The red rose and the briar.

17

THE HOUSE CARPENTER

"Well met, well met, my own true love,
  Well met, well met," says he,
"I've just returned from the salt, salt sea,
  And it's all for the sake of thee.

"I could have married a king's daughter fair,
  And she fain would have married me,
But I refused her crowns of gold,
  And it's all for the sake of thee."

"If you could have married a king's daughter fair,
  I think 'twould have been your plan,
For I have marry-ed a house carpenter,
  And I think him a nice young man."

"If you'll forsake your house carpenter,
   And go along with me,
I'll take you where the grass grows green
   On the banks of Italy."

She called her babe unto her knee,
   And kisses gave it three,
Saying, "Stay at home, you pretty little babe,
   Keep your father's company."

She dressed herself in scarlet red,
   Most glorious to behold,
And as they sailed the ports all round,
   She shone like the glittering gold.

They had not aboard the ship two weeks,
   I'm sure it was not three,
When the fair lady began for to weep,
   And she wept most bitterlally.

"O, is it for my gold that you weep,
   Or is it for my store,
Or is it for your house carpenter,
   Whom you ne'er shall see no more?"

"It is not for your gold that I weep,
   Nor neither for your store,
But I do mourn for the pretty little babe
   That I left on the other shore."

They had not been on board three weeks,
   I'm sure it was not four,
When this gallant ship she sprang a leak,
   And she sank for to rise no more.

A curse, a curse to that young man,
   And a curse to the seaman's life,
A-robbing of the house carpenter
   And a-stealing away his wife!

18

TWO LITTLE BOYS

Two little boys going to school,
   Two little boys they be;
Two little boys going to school
   To learn their A B C.

"O, will you toss a ball with me,
   Or will you throw a stone?
Or will you wrestle along with me
   On the road as we go home?"

"I will not toss a ball with you,
   Nor will I throw a stone,
But I will wrestle along with you,
   On the road as we go home."

They wrestled up, they wrestled down,
    They wrestled around and around,
And a little penknife run through John's pocket,
    And he received a deadly wound.

"Take off, take off my fine cotton shirt,
    And tear it from gore to gore,
And bind it around that bloody bloody wound,
    That it may bleed no more."

So I took off his fine cotton shirt,
    And tore it from gore to gore,
And bound it around that bloody bloody wound,
    So it would bleed no more.

"O what shall I tell your mother, John,
    If she inquires for you?"
"O, tell her I've gone to the royal school
    My books to bring home."

"O what shall I tell your sister, John,
    If she inquires for you?"
"O, tell her I've gone down to the city,
    Some friends for to see."

"O, what shall I tell you true love, John,
    If she inquires for you?"
"O, tell her I'm dead and lying in my grave,
    Way out in Idaho."

19

THE CHERRY TREE CAROL

When Joseph was an old man, an old man was he,
He married Virgin Mary, the Queen of Galilee.

As Joseph and Mary were walking one day
Here are apples, here are cherries, enough to behold.

Then Mary spoke to Joseph so meek and so mild,
"Joseph gather me some cherries, for I am with child."

Then Joseph flew in anger, in anger flew he,
"Let the father of the baby gather cherries for thee."

Then Jesus spoke a few words, a few words spoke He,
"Let my mother have some cherries, bow low down,
    Cherry Tree."

The cherry tree bowed low down, bowed low down
    to the ground,
And Mary gathered cherries while Joseph stood around.

Then Joseph took Mary all on his right knee:
"What have I done—Lord have mercy on me!"

Then Joseph took Mary all on his left knee:
"O tell me little baby, when Thy birthday will be?"

"The sixth day of January my birthday will be,
When the stars in their elements shall tremble with glee."

20

THE FALSE KNIGHT

"Where are you going?" said the false knight, false
knight,
  "Where are you going?" said the false knight Munro.
"Well," said the little boy, "I'm going to school,
But I'll stand to my book al-so."

"What you got in your basket?" said the false knight,
false knight,
  "What you got in your basket?" said the false
  knight Munro.
"Well," said the little boy, "my breakfast and my
  dinner,
But I'll stand to my book al-so."

"Give my dog some," said the false knight Munro.
  "Give my dog some," said false knight Munro.
"Well," said the little boy, "I won't give him none,
But I'll stand to my book al-so."

"Then I'll pitch you in the well," said the false knight
  Munro,
  "Then I'll pitch you in the well," said the false
  knight Munro.
"Well," said the little boy, "I'll pitch you in first,
But I'll stand to my book al-so."

And he pitched him in the well and went on to school.

OTHER IMPORTED
BALLADS AND
SONGS

21

(A) THE DROWSY SLEEPER

"Arouse, arouse, ye drowsy sleepers,
  Arouse, arouse, 'tis almost day.
Open your door, your dining room window,
  And hear what your true lover say."

"What is this that comes under my window,
  A-speaking to me thus speedily?"
"It is your Jimmy, your own true Jimmy,
  A-wanting to speak one word with thee."

"Go away from my window, you'll waken my father,
  For he's taking of his rest.
Under his pillow there lies a weapon
  To pierce the man that I love best.

"Go away from my window, you'll waken my mother,
  For tales of war she will not hear.
Go away and court some other,
  Or whisper lowly in my ear."

"I won't go away and court any other,
  For here I do no harm;
I only want you from your own dear mother,
  To wrap you in your lover's arms.

"I wish I was down in some lonesome valley,
  Where I could neither see nor hear.

My food it should be grief and sorrow,
  My drink it would be the briny tear.

"Down in a valley there lies a sharp arrow,
  I wish I had it across my breast;
It would cut off all grief and sorrow,
  And lay this troubled heart to rest."

(B) WILLIE AND MARY

"O who is at my bedroom window,
  Who weeps and sighs so bitterly. . . .

"O Mary dear, go ask your mother,
  If you my wedded bride may be;
And if she says 'Nay' then come and tell me,
  And I no more will trouble thee."

"O Willie dear, I dare not ask her,
  For she lies on her bed of rest;
And by her side there lies another. . . .

"O, Mary dear, go ask your father,
  If you my wedded bride may be;
And if he says 'Nay' then come and tell me,
  And I no more will trouble thee."

"O Willie dear, I dare not ask him,
  For he is on his bed of rest;
And by his side there lies a dagger
  To pierce the one that I love best."

Then Willie drew a silver dagger
  And pierced it through his aching breast,
Saying, his farewell to his own true lover,
  "Farewell, farewell, I am at rest."

Then Mary drew the bloody dagger
  And pierced it through her snow-white breast,
Saying her farewell, "Dear father, mother,
  Farewell, farewell, we're both at rest."

22

(A) THE BAMBOO BRIARS

One night as they was sitting courting
Two villains overheard,
Saying, "This courtship it shall be ended,
We will send him along to his grave."

And to conclude this bloody murder
A-hunting these two villains did go.

They travelled over hills and hollows
And places too that was not known,
Until they came to the bamboo briars,
And there they killed him—killed and thrown.

It is "Dear brothers, where have you been?
The reason I ask you seems to whisper—
Dear brothers, tell me if you can."

One night as she was lying weeping,
He came to her in gory blood,
Saying, "What do you weep for, you harmless creature?
Your brothers killed me, killed and thrown.

"And was by being both rash and cruel
In such a place you can me find."

She travelled over hills and hollows
And places too that was not known,
Until she came to the bamboo briars,
And there she found him killed and thrown.

She stayed three days, hunger came on her,
Then she returned back home again.

It is, "Dear sister where have you been?
The reason we ask you seems to whisper,
Dear sister, tell us if you can."

"You are two hard-hearted, deceitful villains,
For him alone you both shall swing."
And, dear friends, if you'll believe me,
The raging seas provide their grave.

(B) THE APPRENTICE BOY

In yon post-town there lived a margent,
He had two sons and a daughter fair:

There lived a 'prentice boy about there,
Who was the daughter's dearest dear.

Ten thousand pounds was this gay lady's portion;
She was a fair and a camelite dame;
She loved this young man who crossed the ocean;
He told her how he could be so deslain.

One day they was in the room a-courting;
The oldest brother chanced to hear;
He went and told the other brother,
They would deprive her of her dear.

Her brothers studied on this cruel matter,
Concluded a-hunting they would go,
And with this young man they both would flatter;
A-hunting with them he had to go.

They traveled over high hills and mountains
And through strange places where it were unknown,
Till at length they came to some lonesome valley,
And then they killed him dead and thrown.

All on that evening when they returned,
She asked them where's her servant-man;
"What makes me ask you?" she seems to whisper,
"Dear brothers, tell me if you can."

"He is lost in the wild woods a-hunting;
His face you never more shall see."

"I'll tell you in plain, you're much affronted;
Oh, now will you explain to me."

All on that night while she lay sleeping,
He came and stood at her bed-feet,
All covered o'er in tears a-weeping,
All wallowed o'er in gores of blood.

He says, "My love it's but a folly;
For this is me that you may see—
Your brothers both being rash and cruel—
In such a valley you may find."

All on next morning when she arose,
She dressed herself in silk so fine;
She traveled o'er high hills and mountains
Her own true-lover for to find.

She traveled o'er high hills and mountains
And through strange places where it were unknown,
Till at length she came to some lonesome valley
Till at length she came to a patch of briars,
And there she found him killed and thrown.

His pretty cheeks with blood were dyed;
His lips were bloody as any butcher.
His lips (cheeks) were salty as any brine;
She kissed them over and over a-crying,
"You dearest bosom friend of mine!"

Three days and night she tarried with him,
Till she thought her heart would break with woe,

Until sharp hunger came cropping on her,
Which forced her back home to go.

All on that evening when she returned,
Her brothers asked her where she'd been—
"O ye hard-hearted deceitful devillions,
For him alone you both shall swing."

Her brothers studied on this bloody matter
Concluded the ocean they would sail;
"My friend, I tell you, it's on the morrow
The raging sea there for to sail."

The sea began to roar, I think no wonder
That they two villyons should be cast away;
And broadways they came tosling under;
The sea did open and provide their grave.

23

(A) THE BOSTON BURGLAR

I was born in Boston, a place you all know well,
Brought up by honest parents, the truth to you I'll tell;
Brought up by honest parents and watched most
    tenderly,
Till I became a roving boy at the age of twenty-three.

For burglaring I was taken and I was sent to jail;
My friends they came to bail me out, but it was of no
    avail.

The judge then read my sentence, the clerk he wrote
    it down,
Said, "For seven long and weary years you're going
    to Jefferson town."

To see my aged father come pleading at the bar,
To see my aged mother a-pulling her gray hair,
Yes, pulling those gray locks, my boy, and the tears
    came streaming down,
Said she, "My son, what have you done? You're
    going to Jefferson town."

They put me on board an eastern train one cold and
    stormy day,
And every station that I passed I heard the people say,
"There goes that noted burglar, in iron he's bound
    down,
For robbing of the Boston bank he's going to Jefferson
    town."

There is a girl in Boston, I know she loves me well
If e'er I gain my liberty 'tis with this girl I'll dwell;
If e'er I gain my liberty, bad company I'll shun,
I'll bid adieu to night-walking and also drinking rum.

Come all you jolly fellows, a warning take of me,
And never go night-walking and shun bad company,
For if you do, you'll surely rue, and you'll be sent
    like me,
For robbing of the Boston bank to the penitentiary.

(B) CHARLESTOWN

I was born in Boston city,
A place you all know well,
Brought up by honest parents,
And the truth to you I'll tell,
Brought up by honest parents,
And reared most tenderly,
Till I became a roving lad
At the age of twenty-three.

My character was taken
And I was sent to jail;
My friends they tried to clear me,
But it was of no avail.
The clerk he read the charges,
While Russell wrote it down,
Saying, "For some noted crime, sir,
You are bound for Charlestown."

To see my poor old father
A-raving at the bar,
Likewise my kind old mother,
A-tearing out her hair,
While tearing out those old gray locks,
The tears came rolling down
Saying, "Son, O son, what has thou done?
You're bound for Charlestown."

I was shipped on board of an east-bound]
    train,
One dark December day;

And every station I'd pass through
I'd hear the people say—
"There goes a noted burglar,
In irons he is bound,
And for some noted crime, sir,
He's bound for Charlestown."

There lived in Boston city
A girl that I loved well,
And if ever I gain my liberty
Along with her I'll dwell,
If ever I gain my liberty
Bad company I'll shun
And night-walking and gambling
And likewise all bad rum.

If you that have your liberty
Just keep it while you can,
And act upon the square, my boy
Obey the laws of man;
For if you don't you'll surely rue,
Your fate will surely be,
Six months in the house erect,
Or the penitentiary.

24

(A) THE BUTCHER'S BOY

In Jersey City where I did dwell
A butcher's boy I loved so well;

He courted me my heart away,
And now with me he will not stay.

There is a house in this same town,
Where my true love goes and sits him down,
He takes a strange girl on his knee,
And tells her what he won't tell me.

'Tis grief, 'tis grief, I'll tell you why,
Because she has more gold than I;
Her gold will melt and silver fly,
She'll see the day she's poor as I.

I went upstairs to make my bed,
And nothing to my mother said,
I took a chair and sit me down,
With pen and ink I wrote it down,

On every line I dropped a tear,
While calling home my Willy dear.
Her father he came home that night,
"Where, O where has my daughter gone?"

He went upstairs, the door he broke,
And found her hanging by a rope.
He took his knife to cut her down,
And on her bosom these lines he found:

"O what a foolish girl am I
To kill myself for a butcher's boy.

"Go dig my grave both wide and deep,
Place a marble stone at my head and feet.
Upon my breast a turtle dove
To show the world I died for love."

(B)   THERE IS A TAVERN IN THE TOWN

There is a tavern in the town, in the town,
And there my dear love sits him down, sits him down,
And drinks his wine mid laughter free,
And never, never thinks of me.

> Fare thee well for I must leave thee,
> Do not let this parting grieve thee,
> And remember that the best of friends must
>   part, must part.

> Adieu, adieu, kind friends, adieu,
> I can no longer stay with you, stay with you,
> I'll hang my harp on the weeping willow tree
> And may the world go well with thee.

He left me for a damsel dark, damsel dark,
Each Friday night they used to spark, used to spark,
And now my love once true to me
Takes that dark damsel on his knee.

O dig my grave both wide and deep, wide and deep,
Put tombstones at my head and feet, head and feet,
And on my breast carve a turtle dove
To signify I died of love.

25
THE DEATH OF A ROMISH LADY

There lived a Romish lady
    Brought up in proper array;
Her mother ofttimes told her
    She must the priest obey.

"O pardon me dear mother
    I humbly pray thee now
For unto these false idols
    I can no longer bow."

Assisted by her handmaid,
    Her bible she concealed
And there she gained instruction
    Till God his love revealed.

No longer would she prostrate
    The pictures decked with gold;
But soon she was betrayed
    Her bible from her stold.

"I'll bow to my dear Jesus
    And worship him unseen
And work by faith unfailing
    The works of men are vain.

"I can not worship idols
    Nor pictures made by men
Dear mother use your pleasure
    But pardon if you can."

With grief and great veration
    Her mother straight did go
To inform the Romish clergy
    The source of all her woe.

The priests was soon assembled
    And for the maid did call.
They forced her in a dungeon
    To affright her soul withal.

The more they strove to affright her
    The more she did endure
Although her age was tender
    Her faith was firm and sure.

Her chains of gold so costly
    They from the lady took
And she with all her spirit
    The pride of life forsook.

Before the priests they brought her
    In hope of her return
But there she was ordained
    In horrid flames to burn.

Before the place of torment
    They brought her speedily.
With lifted hands to heaven
    She there agreed to die.

There being many ladies
　　Assembled at that place,
With lifted hands to heaven
　　She begged supporting grace.

"Weep not ye tender ladies,
　　Shed not a tear for me
Whilst my poor body's burning
　　My soul the Lord shall see.

"Yourselves you need to pity
　　On Zion's deep decay.
Dear ladies, turn to Jesus
　　No longer make delay."

In comes her raging mother,
　　Her daughter to behold;
And in her hand she brought
　　An image decked with gold.

"O take from me those idols
　　Remove them from my sight.
Restore to me my Bible
　　In which I take delight.

"Alas, my aged mother
　　On my ruin bent,
It was her that did betray me;
　　But I am innocent.

"Tormentors, use your pleasure
 And do as you think best.
I hope my blessed Jesus
 Will take me home to rest."

Soon as these words were spoken
 In comes the tyrant of death,
And kindled up the fire
 To stop her mortal breath.

Instead of gold and bracelets,
 With chains they bound her fast;
She cried aloud, "O Lord, give pardon,
 Or else I sink at last.

"With Jesus and his angels
 For ever I shall dwell.
God pardon priest and people
 And so I bid farewell."

26

JOHNNY AND BETSY

There was an old woman who lived on the strand,
And Johnny was her only son,
And servant Betsy, beauty fair,
Drew his heart into a snare.
One evening Johnny took his time
To tell to her what was in his mind:

"O Betsy, O Betsy, I love you well!
I love you better than tongue can tell!
O Betsy, O Betsy, I love you dear!"

His mother chanced these words to hear.
Then she resolved within her mind
To stop these two of their designs.
Early next morning when she arose
She says to Betsy, "Put on your clothes.
Go dress yourself," says she,
"And wait on me two days or three."

Then o'er the country they went,
But Betsy knew not her intent.
There was a ship lying in the down,
And to Verginny it was bound,
Where she sold Betsy across the main,
And returned safe home to her son again.

"You're welcome home, dear mother," he says,
"But where is Betsy behind you stayed?"
"O son, O son, your love's in vain,
For we sold Betsy 'cross the main.
My son, my son," says she,
"You're bringing scandal on you and me.
I would rather see your corpse lie dead
Than to marry Betsy, a servant maid."

"Then your desire you soon shall have,
If you'd rather see my corpse lie dead

Than to marry Betsy, a servant maid!"
Then he took sick, O very bad,
No mirth nor music could make him glad.
They sent for doctors far and near,
But none of them could Johnny cheer;
And every doctor tried their skill
Till at last they did poor Johnny kill.

And when she saw her son lie dead,
She rang her hands and tore her head,
Saying, "If life I once could bring again,
I'd send for Betsy across the main!
If life I once could bring again,
I would send for Betsy across the main!"

27

THE SOLDIER

I once knew a soldier just from the war,
He courted a lady for honor and for store;
The lady loved the soldier because he was so bold.
So great was her fortune it scarcely could be told.

"Now," said the lady, "I cannot be your wife,
For fear my wretched father would shortly end your
    life."
He drew a sword and pistol and hung them by his side
Saying, "We will get married and who will betide."

They went and got married and coming back again,
They met the wretched father with several armed men.
"Let's flee," said the lady, "for fear we will be killed."
"Hold on," said the soldier, "at fighting I am skilled."

Up stepped the old man, speaking very free,
Saying, "Do you intend to be a daughter unto me,
Or do you intend to be a soldier's wife?
Then in this lonesome valley I'll shortly end your life."

"Now," said the soldier, "I have no time to tattle,
I'm only one alone but I'm ready for the battle."
He drew his sword and pistol and caused them both to
    rattle.
The lady held the horses while the soldier fought the
    battle.

The first one he came to he run him through the brain,
The next one he came to he served him just the same.
"Hold on," said the old man, "Don't strike so bold,
And you can have my daughter and ten thousand
    pounds of gold."

28

THE FARMER'S BOY

The sun had set behind the hill across the dreary moor,
When weary and lame a poor boy came up to a farmer's
    door.

"Pray tell to me if any there be to give to me employ,
To plow and sow, to reap and mow, and to be a farmer's
    boy.

"My father's dead, my mother's left five children very
    small,
And what is worse for mother still I'm the eldest of
    them all,
Though little I be I fear no work if you will me employ,
To plow to sow, to reap and mow and to be a farmer's
    boy.

"And if you will not me employ a favor I have to ask.
Will you shelter me till the break of day from this cold
    winter's blast?
At the break of day I'll haste away elsewhere to seek
    employ
To plow, to sow, to reap and mow, and to be a farmer's
    boy."

The farmer said, "Pray take the lad, no farther let him
    seek."
"O yes, dear father," the daughter cried, while tears
    ran down her cheek,
Those that will work 'tis hard to want and wander for
    employ,
To plow, to sow, to reap, to mow, and be a farmer's
    boy.

In course of time he grew to be a man.   This good old
    farmer died,

And he left the lad the farm he had and the daughter
 for his bride.
Now the lad that was the farmer is, he oft times thinks
 with joy
Of the lucky day he came that way to be a farmer's boy,
To plow, to sow, to reap and mow, and to be a farmer's
 boy.

29

THE RICH YOUNG FARMER

There was a rich young farmer,
 And he was of high renown,
He courted a fair and handsome daughter,
 As ever lived in England town.

When her parents came to know it,
 It grieved their hearts full sore;
They said they'd send him far over the ocean,
 Where he'd cease to love no more.

One morning, O one morning,
 One morning just at dawn,
As bold as a ranger and just like a stranger
 I met my true love a-walking along.

"Look up, look up, my pretty fair maiden,
 O can't you fancy me?"
"O no, kind sir, my fancy is a farmer,
 And has lately gone to sea."

"Describe him, O describe him,
  Describe him unto me;
For perhaps I saw a sword pass through him,
  As I've lately been to sea."

"He is proper, neat, and handsome,
  He is proper, neat, and tall,
He has long black hair and he wears it platted,
  Through a gay gold ring doth fall."

"O yes, I saw him, and I know him,
  His name is Thomas Hall;
I saw a cannon ball pass through him,
  And thus, fair lady, your lover did fall."

She stood wringing her lily white hands,
  As though her heart would break.
"Hush up, hush up, my pretty fair maiden,
  Perhaps I be the very man."

She turned around and looked upon him,
  She turned and looked again.
She hopped and she flew and she ran unto him,
  And embraced him by the hand.

They joined their loving hands together,
  And straight to the church did go,
And married they never must each other,
  Whether their parents were willing or no.

30

THE LOVER'S RETURN

It was on one munday morning in may
  Down by a flowery garden I chanced for to stray
I over heard a fair maid with sorrow to complain
  All on the banks of clowdy I am told she doth remain.

I stepped away unto her I took her with surprise
  She owned she did not now me for I was in disguise
Oh my handsom fair maid my joy and hearts delight
  How far have you to ramble this dark and rainy night

Kind sir away to clowdy would you be pleased to show
  Be kind unto a fair miss for there I haf to go
I am on the search for a young man and Ione is his name
  All on the banks of clowdy I am told he doth remain.

It's on the banks of clowdy on which you boldly stand
  For dont you believe young Ione for he will not meet
    you
  O dont you believe young Ione for he is a faulse young
    man
    So stay with me in the green groves no danger need
    fear.

If Ione he was here this night he would keep me from
    all harm
  But he is in the field of battle dressed in his uniform

He is in the field of Battle his foes he doth defy
 He is like the kings of honor he is in the wars to try

It has been six months or better since Ione left the shore
 A sailing the wide ocian where raging billows rore
A sailing the wide ocian with horror and great gain
 The ship has been recked as I have been told all on
  the cost of Spain.

When she heard this dreadful she sunk into dispair
 A ringing of her hands and a taring of her hair
Saying if Ione he is drowned no other will I take
 In some lonesome grove or vally I will die for his sake.

When he beheld her royalty he could no longer stand
 He flew into her arms crying Betsy I am the man
I am your royal true love the cause of all your pain
 And since we have met on clowdy's banks we never
  shall part again.

31

THE PRENTICE BOY

As low in Cupid's garden for pleasure I did walk
I heard two loyal lovers most sweetly for to talk
It was a briske yong lady and her prentice boy
And in private they were courting and he was all her
 joy

He said dear honord lady I am your prentice boy
How ever can I thinke a fair lady to enjoy

His cheeks as red as roses his humor kind and free
She said dear youth if ever I wed I'll surely mary thee.

But when her parents came this for to understand
They did this young man banish to some foreign land
While she lay broken hearted lamenting she did cry
For my honest charming prentice a maid I'll live and die

This young man to a merchant a waiting man was
    bound
And by his good behaviour good fortune there he found
He soon became his butler which prompted him to faim
And for his careful conduct the steward he became

For a ticket in a lottery his money he put down
And there he gained a prize of twenty thousand pound
With store of gold and silver he packed up his close
    indeed
And to England returned to his true love with speed

He offered kind embraces but she flew from his arms
No lord duke or nobleman shall ever endure my charms
The love of gold is cursed great riches I decry
For my honest charming prentice a maid I'll live and
    and die

He said dear honord lady I have been in your arms
This is the ring you gave me for toying in your charms
You vowed if every you maried your love I should
    enjoy
Your father did me banish I was your prentice boy

When she beheld his features she flew into his arms
With kisses out of measure she did enjoy his charms
Then so through Cupid's garden a road to church they
    found
And there in virtuous pleasure in hymen's band was
    bound.

32

THE CONSTANT FARMER'S SON

There was a farmer's daughter near Dublin town did
    dwell,
So modest, fair and handsome, her parents loved her
    well;
She was admired by lord and dukes, but all their hopes
    were vain.
There was but one, a farmer's son, young Mary's heart
    could gain.

Long time young Willie courted her and fixed their
    wedding day;
Her parents both they gave consent, but her brothers
    they did say:
"There lives a lord that pledged his word, and if you
    do him shun,
We will betray and then will slay your constant farmer's
    son."

There was a fair not far from home, her brothers went
    straightway

And asked Willie's company to pass the time away.
But, mark, returning home at night they swore his
    race was run,
And with a stake the life did take of her constant
    farmer's son.

As Mary on her pillow lay she dreamed a dismal dream,
She dreamt she saw her true love's gore; the blood
    appeared in streams;
She then arose, put on her clothes, to seek her love did
    run,
When dead and cold she did behold her constant
    farmer's son.

The bitter tears ran down her cheeks and mingled with
    his gore,
She cried in vain to ease her pain and kissed him o'er
    and o'er;
She gathered green leaves from off the trees to shade
    him from the sun,
And one night and day was passed away with her
    constant farmer's son.

But hunger it came creeping on, poor girl she cried with
    woe,
And for to find his murderers she straightway home did
    go,
Saying, "Parents dear, you soon shall hear of a shocking
    deed that's done.
In yonder vale lies dead and pale my constant farmer's
    son."

Then up bespoke her eldest brother, saying, "Indeed
   it was not me."
The same replied her youngest brother and cursed most
   bitterly.
"Brothers," she said, "don't turn so red or try the law
   to shun;
You did the deed and sore you will bleed for my constant farmer's son."

These villains then did own their guilt and for the same
   did die;
Young Mary fair in deep despair, she never ceased to
   cry;
Her parents both they vanished away for their span of
   life was run;
Young Mary cried and of sorrow died for her constant
   farmer's son.

33

MOLLIE BOND

Come all you young men who handle a gun,
Be warned of shooting after the down sun.

A story I'll tell you; it happened of late,
Concerning Mollie Bond, whose beauty was great.

Mollie Bond was out walking, and a shower came on;
She sat under a beech tree the showers to shun.

Jim Random was out hunting, a-hunting in the dark;
He shot at his true love and missed not his mark.

With a white apron pinned around her he took her for
   a swan,
He shot and killed her, and it was Mollie Bond.

He ran to her; these words to her he said;
And a fountain of tears on her bosom he shed.

Saying, "Mollie, dear Mollie, you're the joy of my life;
I always intended to make you my wife."

Jim ran to his uncle with his gun in his hand,
Saying, "Uncle, dear uncle, I've killed Mollie Bond.

"With her apron pinned around her, I took her for a
   swan;
I shot and killed her, and it was Mollie Bond."

Up stepped his dear uncle with his locks all so gray,
Saying, "Stay at home, Jimmie, and do not run away.

"Stay in your own country till your trial comes on;
You shall not be molested if it costs me my farm."

The day of Jimmy's trial Mollie's ghost did appear,
Saying to this jury, "Jim Random come clear!

"With my apron pinned around me he took me for a
   swan,
He shot and killed me and now I am gone."

34

MY FATHER'S GRAY MARE

Young Roger the miller went courting of late
A farmer's fair daughter called Kate.

Her cheeks like vermilion all painted with love,
She was buxom and bonny and sweet as a dove.

Then Roger being greedy, I do declare,
He spied the nag they called the gray mare.

"As for your daughter I solemnly swear,
I won't have your daughter without the gray mare."

The old man rose up with anger and speed,
"I thought you'd have married my daughter indeed.

"But since it is so I am glad it is thus,
My money once more I'll put up in my purse.

"As for my daughter I solemnly swear
You can't have my daughter, no nor the gray mare."

When six months were ended, or something above
Young Roger he chanced to meet with his love.

"O," smiling, said Roger, "and don't you know me?"
"If I ain't mistaken, I've seen you," said she.
"A man of your likeness, with long yellow hair,
Did once come a-courting my father's gray mare."

35

MARY O' THE WILD MOOR

'Twas on a cold winter's night
  When the wind blew across the wild moor,
That Mary came wandering home with her child,
  Till she came to her own father's door.
"O father, dear father," she cried,
  "Come down and open the door,
Or the child in my arms will perish and die,
  By the winds that blow 'cross the wild moor."

"O why did I leave this dear cot,
  Where once I was happy and free?
But now I must roam without friends or home,
  No one to take pity on me!"
Her father was deaf to her cries,
  Not a sound of her voice reached his ear;
But the watch dog he howled and the village bell
    tolled,
  And the winds blew across the wild moor.

O how must that old man have felt
  When he came to the door in the morn;
Poor Mary was dead, but her child was alive,
  Closely pressed in its dead mother's arms.

Half frantic he tore his gray hair,
  And the tears down his cheeks they did pour,
For on that bitter night she had perished and died,
  From the winds that blew 'cross the wild moor.

The old man in grief pined away,
  And the child to its mother went soon;
And no one, they say, has lived there to this day,
  And the cottage to ruin has gone.
The villagers point to the spot
  Where the ivy hangs over the door,
Saying, "There Mary died, once a gay village bride,
  By the winds that blow 'cross the wild moor."

36

FATHER GRUMBLE

Father Grumble he did say,
  As sure as the moss round a tree,
That he could do more work in a day
  Than his wife could do in three, three,
  Than his wife could do in three.

Then Mother Grumble she did say,
  "O what's the row now?
You can stay in the house and work,
  And I will follow the plow, plow,
  And I will follow the plow.

"But don't forget the jar of cream
    That stands within the frame, frame;
And don't forget the fat in the pot,
    Or it will go into flame, flame;
And don't forget the fat in the pot,
    Or it will all go into flame.

"Don't forget the muley-cow,
    For fear she will go dry, dry;
And don't forget the little pigs
    That lie within the sty, sty;
And don't forget the little pigs
    That lie within the sty.

"Don't forget the speckled hen,
    For fear she'll lay astray, astray;
And don't forget the skein of yarn
    That I spin every day, day;
And don't forget the skein of yarn
    That I spin every day."

He went to churn the jar of cream
    That stood within the frame, frame;
And he forgot the fat in the pot,
    And it all went into flame, flame;
And he forgot the fat in the pot,
    And it all went into flame.

He went to milk the muley-cow,
    For fear she would go dry, dry;

She reared, she kicked, she faunched, she flinched,
  She hit him over the eye, eye;
She reared, she kicked, she faunched, she flinched,
  She hit him over the eye.

He went to watch the speckled hen,
  For fear she'd lay astray, astray;
And he forgot the skein of yarn
  That she spun every day;
And he forgot the skein of yarn
  That she spun every day.

Old Father Grumble coming in
  And looking very sad, sad,
Old Mother Grumble clapped her hands
  And said that she was very glad, glad;
Old Mother Grumble clapped her hands
  And said that she was very glad.

37

GUY FAWKES

I'll tell you a doleful tragedy—
  Guy Fawkes, the prince of sinisters,
Who once blew up the House of Lords,
  The King and all his ministers;
That is, he would have blown them up,
  And we would ne'er forget him,

His will was good to do the deed,
   If they had only let him.

     Singing bow—wow—wow,
     Whack fol—de—riddle,
     Singing bow—wow—wow.

Straightway he came from Lambeth side
   And wished the State was undone;
And crossing over Vauxhall bridge
   That way he came to London;
That is, he would have crossed the bridge
   To perpetrate his guilt, sir,
But a trifling thing prevented him,
   The bridge it was not built, sir.

And as he searched the dreary vaults
   With portable gas light, sir,
About to touch the powder train
   At the witching hour of night, sir;
That is, he would have used the gas,
   Had he not been prevented;
But gas you know, in James's time,
   It hadn't been invented.

Now, when they caught him in the act,
   So very near the Crown's end,
They sent straightway to Bow Street for
   That gay old runner Townsend;
That is, they would have sent for him

For danger he's no starter at,
But Townsend wasn't living then,
He wasn't born till arter that.

So then they put poor Guy to death
For ages to remember;
And now they kill him every year
In dreary dark November;
That is, his effigy, I mean,
For truth is strange and steady,
They cannot put poor Guy to death
For he is dead already.

38

WILLIAM REILLY'S COURTSHIP

'Twas on a pleasant morning all in the bloom of spring
When as the cheerful songsters in concert sweet did
sing,
The primrose and the daisy bespangled every dawn
In an arbor I espied my dear Coolen Bawn.

I stood awhile amazed, quite struck with surprise,
On her with rapture gazed while from her bright eyes
She shot such killing glances my heart away was drawn.
She ravished all my senses, my fair Coolen Bawn.

I tremblingly addressed her: "Hail, matchless fair maid!
You have with grief oppressed me and I am much
afraid.

Except you'll cure my anguish which now is in its dawn,
  You'll cause my sad overthrow, my sweet Coolen
  Bawn."

Then with a gentle smile she replied unto me.
  "I cannot tyrannize, dear Willie, over thee.
My father he is wealthy and gives severe command;
  If you but gain his favor, I'll be your Coolen Bawn."

In raptures I embrace her; we swore eternal love,
  And nought should separate us except the power
  above.
I hired with her father and left my friends and land
  That with pleasure I might gaze on my fair Coolen
  Bawn.

I served him twelve months right faithful and just,
  Although not used to labor, was true to my trust.
I valued not my wages, I would not it demand,
  For I could live for ages with my Coolen Bawn.

One morning as her father and I walked out alone,
  I asked him for his daughter saying: "Sir, it is well
  known
I have a well-stocked farm, five hundred pound in hand
  Which I'll share with your daughter, my fair Coolen
  Bawn."

Her father full of anger most scornfully did frown,
  Saying, "Here are your wages. Now, sir, depart
  from this town."

Increasing still his anger he bid me quick begone,
"For none but a rich squire shall wed my Coolen
Bawn."

I went unto his daughter and told her my sad tale.
Oppressed with grief and anger we both did weep
and wail.
She said, "My dearest Reilly, the thought I can't
withstand
That in your sorrow you should leave me, your own
dear Coolen Bawn."

A horse I did get ready in the silent night.
Having no other remedy, we quickly took our flight.
The horse he chanced to stumble and threw both along,
Confused and solely bruised me and my dear Coolen
Bawn

Again we quickly mounted and swiftly rode away.
O'er hills and lofty mountains we travelled night
and day.
Her father quickly pursued us with his well chosen
band,
And I was overtaken with my fair Coolen Bawn.

Committed straight to prison there to lament and wail,
And utter my complaints to a dark and dismal jail,
Loaded with heavy irons till my trial should come on,
But I'll bear their utmost malice for my dear Coolen
Bawn.

If it should please kind fortune once more to set me free,
  For well I know my charmer is constant unto me,
Spite of her father's anger, his cruelty and scorn,
  I hope to wed my heart's delight, my dear Coolen
  Bawn.

39

JACK RILEY

Jack Riley is my true love's name;
  He lives down by the sea,
And he is as nice a young man
  As e'er my eyes did see.

My father he is rich and great,
  Jack Riley he is poor;
And because I loved my sailor boy
  He would not me endure.

My mother took me by the hand;
  These words to me did say,
"If you be fond of Riley,
  You must leave this counteray.

"For your father says he will take his life,
  And that without delay.
So you must either go abroad,
  Or shun his company."

"O mother dear, don't be severe.
  Where shall I send my love?
For if father kills Jack Riley
  I will meet him up above."

"O daughter dear, I'm not severe.
  Here is one thousand pounds.
Send Riley to Amerikay,
  To purchase there some grounds."

NATIVE BALLADS
AND SONGS

40

THE BATTLE OF POINT PLEASANT

Let us mind the tenth day of October,
  Seventy-four, which caused woe.
The Indian savages they did cover
  The pleasant banks of the Ohio.

Colonel Lewis and some noble Captains,
  Did down to death like Uriah go.
Alas! their heads are bound up with napkins,
  Upon the banks of the Ohio.

Seven score lay dead and wounded,
  Of champions who did face the foe;
By which the heathen were confounded,
  Upon the banks of the Ohio.

Oh, bless the mighty king of heaven,
  For all his wondrous works below,
Who hath to us the victory given
  Upon the banks of the Ohio.

41

JAMES BIRD

Sons of pleasure, listen to me,
  And ye daughters, too, give ear,
You a sad and mournful story
  As was ever told shall hear.

Hull, you know, his troops surrendered,
    And defenseless left the West,
Then our forces quick assembled,
    This invader to resist.

Among the troops that marched to Erie,
    Were the Kingston volunteers;
Captain Thomas then commanded
    To protect our West frontiers.

Tender was the scene of parting—
    Mothers wrung their hands and cried,
Maidens wept their love in secret,
    Fathers strove their tears to hide.

But there was one among that number,
    Tall and graceful in his mien.
Firm his steps, his looks undaunted—
    Ne'er a nobler youth was seen.

One sweet kiss he snatched from Mary,
    Begged his mother's prayers once more,
Pressed his father's hand and left them
    For Lake Erie's distant shore.

Mary strove to say, "Farewell, James!"
    Waved her hand but nothing spoke;
"Good-bye, Bird! May Heaven protect you."
    From the rest the parting broke.

Soon they came where noble Perry
    Had assembled all his fleet;
There the gallant Bird enlisted,
    Hoping soon the foe to meet.

Where is Bird?   The battle rages;
    Is he in the strife or no?
Now the cannon roar tremendous,
    Dare he meet the furious foe?

Ah behold him.   See! with Perry
    In the selfsame ship he fights;
Though his messmates fall around him,
    Nothing can his soul affright.

But, behold, a ball hath struck him!
    See the crimson current flow;
"Leave the deck," exclaimed brave Perry.
    "No," cried Bird, "I will not go.

"Here on deck I've took my station.
    Ne'er will Bird his colors fly.
I'll stand by the gallant Captain
    Till we conquer or we die!"

So he fought both faint and bleeding,
    Till our stars and stripes arose,
Victory having crowned our efforts,
    All triumphant o'er our foes.

And did Bird receive a pension?
  Was he to his friends restored?
No, nor even to his bosom
  Clasped the maid whom he adored.

But there came most dismal tidings
  From Lake Erie's distant shore;
Better if poor Bird had perished
  Amid the battle's awful roar.

"Dearest parents," said the letter,
  "This will bring sad news to you.
Do not mourn your first beloved,
  Though this brings his last adieu.

"I must suffer for deserting
  From the brig Niagara;
Read this letter, brother, sister.
  'Tis the last you will hear from me."

Sad and gloomy was the morning
  Bird was ordered out to die;
Where is the breast dares not to pity
  Or for him would heave one sigh?

O he fought so brave at Erie.
  Nobly bled and nobly dared,
Let his courage plead for mercy—
  Let his precious life be spared!

See him march; hear his fetters
　　Harsh they clash upon the ear;
But his step is firm and manly,
　　For his breast ne'er harbored fear.

See, he kneels upon his coffin,
　　Sure his death can do no good;
Spare Him! Hark! O God, they have shot
　　him,
　　See his bosom streams with blood.

Farewell, Bird, farewell forever!
　　Friends and home you'll see no more;
But his mangled corpse lies buried
　　On Lake Erie's distant shore.

42

(A) O JOHNNY DEAR, WHY DID YOU GO?

In Conway town there did dwell
A lovely youth I knew full well.

　　　Ri tu nic a neari
　　　Ri tu nic a neari na.

One day this youth did go
Down in the meadow for to mow.

He mowed all around, at length did feel
A pizen serpent bite his heel.

They carried him to Betsy dear,
Which made her feel so very queer.

"O Johnny dear, why did you go
Down in the meadow for to mow?"

"O Betsy dear I thought you knowed
'Twas daddy's hay and must be mowed."

Now this young man gave up the ghost
And away to Abraham's bosom post.

(B)   [WOODVILLE MOUND]

Near Woodville Mound there did dwell
A lovely youth, I knew him well.
'Twas Deacon Jones' oldest son,
Who just riz up from twenty-one.

    Sing fal dum diddle, fal dum a day
    Fal dum diddle dum a day.

John he went down in the wheatfield
And a mighty big snake bit him on the heel.

*   *   *   *   *   *   *   *
*   *   *   *   *   *   *   *

"O, Dad," said John, "run for my gal;
I'm going to die, I know I shall."

And Dad he went and carried the news
And here come Sal without her shoes.

"O John," said Sal, "why did you go
Down in that wheatfield for to mow?"
"O Sal," said John, "I thought you knowed
That Daddy's wheat had for to be mowed."

(C)   IN SPRINGFIELD MOUNTAIN

In Springfield Mountain there did dwell
     Come-a-row
In Springfield Mountain there did dwell
A lovely couple that I love so well.
     Come-a-rousing-a-tousing-tudan-an-a-die.

He went out in the meadow for to mow,
When a garter snake gathered him by the toe.

He mowed just twice around the field
When a rattle-snake gathered him by the heel.

O, he stepped back as he thought best
Right into a yaller-jacket's nest.

"O, Billie dear, why did you go
Out in the meadow for to mow?"

"O, Mary dear, I thought you knowed
'Twas your pa's hay and it had to be mowed."

(D) SPRINGFIELD MOUNTAIN

Near Springfield Mountain there did dwell
   Tum er ei tum too tum tidinei ay
Near Springfield Mountain there did dwell.
   Tumerow.

Near Springfield Mountain there did dwell
   Tum er ei, etc.
A lovelie youth was known full well,
   Tumerow.

This lovelie youth was sixty-one
   Tum er ei, etc.
And General Jackson's favorite son,
   Tumerow.

This lovelie youth courting one night
   Tum er ei, etc.
Got into a tremendous fight
   Tumerow.

One Sunday morning he did go
   Tum er ei, etc.
Down in the meadows for to mow.
   Tumerow.

43

(A) THE JEALOUS LOVER

Way down in the lonely valley,
 Where the violets fade and bloom,
'Tis there my sweet Lorella
 Lies mouldering in the tomb.
She did not stay heartbroken,
 Nor by disease she fell,
But in one moment parted
 From those she loved so well.

  The banners waved above her,
   Shrill was the bugle sound,
  But strangers came and found her
   Cold, lifeless on the ground.

One night when the moon shone brightly,
 And the stars were shining too,
Into her quiet cottage
 Her jealous lover drew,
Saying, "Love, come let us wander
 Amid the fields so gay;
While wandering we will ponder
 Upon our wedding day."

Deep, deep into the woodland,
 He drew his love so dear;
Says she, " 'Tis for you only

That I am wandering here.
The day grows dark and dreary,
    And I'm afraid to stay;
Of wandering I am weary,
    And we'll retrace my way."

"Retrace your steps?   No, never!
    No more this world you roam,
So bid farewell forever
    To your parents, friends, and home."
"Farewell, my loving parent;
    I ne'er shall see you more;
Long, long will be my coming
    To the quiet cottage door."

Down on her knees before him
    She begged him for her life;
Deep, deep into her bosom,
    He plunged the fatal knife,
"Dear Willie, I'll forgive you,"
    Was her last dying breath;
"I never have deceived you,"
    She closed her eyes in death.

(B) THE WEEPING WILLOW

Way down in yonder valley,
    Where the weeping willows wave,
There lies my poor Lurella
    In her cold and silent grave.

She died not broken hearted,
   From sickness or despair,
But in one moment started
   From the friends she loved so fair—

Down on her knees before him
   She pleaded for her life;
But deep into her bosom
   He plunged the fatal knife.

Saying, "Your parents will forgive me
   For the deed which I have done;
For I'm going to leave this country
   Never more for to return."

44

YOUNG CHARLOTTE

Young Charlotte lived on the mountain side
   In a lone and dreary spot;
No other house for miles around
   Except her father's cot.

And yet on many a winter's night,
   Young swains were gathered there;
For her father kept a social board,
   And she was very fair.

Her father loved to see her dressed
  Like any city belle;
She was the only child he had
  And he loved his daughter well.

On New Year's eve as the sun went down,
  Far looked her wistful eye
Out from the frosty window pane
  As the merry sleighs passed by.

In the village fifteen miles away,
  Was to be a ball that night,
And though the air was piercing cold
  Her heart beat warm and light.

How brightly beams her laughing eye,
  As a well-known voice she hears;
And driving up to the cottage door
  Young Charles and his sleigh appears.

"O daughter dear," her mother said,
  "This blanket round you fold;
It is a dreadful night without,
  You'll catch your death of cold."

"O no, O no!" young Charlotte cried,
  And she laughed like a gypsy queen;
"To ride in blankets muffled up,
  I never will be seen.

My silken cloak is quite enough,
  You know it's lined throughout;
Besides I have my silken scarf
  To tie my neck about."

Her bonnet and her gloves put on,
  She stepped into the sleigh,
Rode swiftly down the mountain side
  And o'er the hills away.

There was music in the sound of the bells,
  As o'er the hills they go;
Such a creaking noise the runners make
  As they cleave the frozen snow.

With muffled face and silent lips
  Five miles at length were passed
When Charles with few and shivering words
  The silence broke at last.

"Such a dreadful night I never knew,
  My reins I scarce can hold.
Fair Charlotte shivering faintly said
  "I am exceeding cold."

He cracked his whip, he urged his steed
  Much faster than before.
And thus five other dreary miles
  In silence they passed o'er.

Says Charles, "How fast the freezing ice
Is gathering on my brow."
And Charlotte still more faintly said
"I'm growing warmer now."

So on they rode through frosty air
And the glittering cold starlight,
Until at last the village lamps
And the ballroom came in sight.

Charles drove to the door, he then jumped out,
And reached his hand for her.
Why sit there like a monument that has no power
to stir?
That has no power to stir?

He called her once, he called her twice;
She answered not a word.
He asked her for her hand again,
But still she never stirred.

He took her hand in his—O God!
'Twas cold and hard as stone.
He tore the mantle from her brow
Cold sweat upon there shone.

Then quickly to the dancing hall
Her lifeless form he bore;
Fair Charlotte was a frozen corpse
And spake she nevermore.

And then he sat down by her side
  While bitter tears did flow,
And cried, "My own, my charming bride,
  You never more will know."

He twined his arms around her neck
  And kissed her marble brow;
His thoughts flew back to where she said
  "I'm growing warmer now."

'Twas then that cruel monster, Death,
  Had claimed her as his own;
Young Charlotte's eyes were closed for aye,
  Her voice was heard no more.

He carried her out to the sleigh,
  And with her he rode home;
And when he reached the cottage door
  O how her parents mourned.

Her parents mourned for their daughter dear,
  And Charles wept o'er the gloom.
Till at last young Charles too died of grief
  And they both lie in one tomb.

Young ladies, think of this fair girl
  And always dress aright,
And never venture thinly clad
  On such a wintry night.

45

(A) THE OLD SHAWNEE

I ask my love to take a walk,
  To take a walk a little way;
And as we walk we'll sweetly talk
  Of when shall be the wedding day.

   Then only say that you'll be mine,
     And your home shall happy be,
  Where the silent waters roll,
     On the banks of the old Shawnee.

She said, "To that I'll ne'er consent,"
  And he says, "Your life I'll take."
"My life you'll take instead of me,
  For I ne'er shall give away."

He drew a knife across her breast,
  And in anger she did cry,
"O Willie dear, don't murder me,
  For I am not fit to die."

He took her by her long black hair,
  And he threw her on the ground,
And drew her to the river side,
  And left her alone to die

(B) ON THE BANKS OF THE OLD PEDEE

I asked my love to take a walk,
   And a walk she took with me.
As we walked I gently talked
   Of when our wedding day would be.

Then she said she'd never be mine,
   And her home would never be
Where the bright waters flow
   On the banks of the old Pedee.

From my breast I drew a knife,
   And she gave a shrilling cry,
"O Willie dear, don't murder me,
   For I am not prepared to die."

Then I took her lily white hands
   And swung her round and again around,
Until she fell in the waters cruel,
   And there I watched my true love drown.

"O father dear, I've done a deed,
   And a deed it is to me,
To have drowned my own true love
   On the banks of the old Pedee."

46

THE MAN THAT WOULDN'T HOE CORN

I'll sing you a song, it won't take long,
Concerning a man who wouldn't hoe corn.
The reason why I cannot tell,
For this young man was always well.

In the month of May he planted his corn,
And in July it was knee high.
In September there came a frost,
The seed of his corn this young man lost.

He went to the fence, peeped in with a grin,
The chick-a-pie weeds were up to his chin.
The weeds and grass had grown so high,
It almost made this young man cry.

Then off to a neighbor's house he goes,
Courting, as we all suppose;
And in the chat as chance came round,
She says, "Young man, have you hoed your
    ground?"

"O no, my dear, I've laid it by,
I thought it was no use to try,
I thought it folly to labor in vain,
When I saw I could raise no grain."

"Then why so silly as to ask me to wed,
When you can't earn your own corn bread?
Single I am and single I'll remain,
A lazy man I won't maintain."

"I won't be bound, I will be free,
I won't marry a man that don't love me;
Neither will I act the childish part,
And marry a man that will break my heart."

He hung his head as he went away,
Saying, "Young woman, you'll rue the day,
Rue the day as sure as you're born,
To give me the mitten because I wouldn't hoe
    corn."

47

(A) WICKED POLLY

Young people, who delight in sin,
I'll tell you what has lately been,
A woman who was young and fair
Has lately died in dark despair.

She would to frolic, dance, and play
In spite of all her friends could say.
"I'll turn to God when I get old,
And then he will receive my soul."

On Friday morning she took sick,
Her stubborn heart began to break
"Alas, alas, my days are spent!
Good lord, too late for to repent!"

She called her mother to her bed;
Her eyes were rolling in her head.
"When I am dead remember well
Your wicked Polly screams in hell!

"The tears are lost you shed for me.
My soul is lost I plainly see.
The flowing wrath begins to roll,
I am a lost, a ruined soul!"

She gnawed her tongue before she died,
She rolled, she groaned, she cried,
Saying, "Must I burn forevermore
When thousand, thousand years are o'er?"

At length master death prevailed.
Her face turned blue, her language failed.
She closed her eyes and left this world.
Poor Polly thought that hell was hers.

This almost broke her mother's heart
To see her child to hell depart.
"My Polly, O my Polly's dead!
Her soul is gone, her spirit's fled!"

(B) WICKED POLLY

O young people, hark while I relate
The story of poor Polly's fate!
She was a lady young and fair
And died a-groaning in despair.

She would go to balls and dance and play
In spite of all her friends could say;
"I'll turn" said she, "when I am old,
And God will then receive my soul."

One Sabbath morning she fell sick;
Her stubborn heart began to ache.
She cries, "Alas my days are spent!
It is too late now to repent."

She called her mother to her bed,
Her eyes were rolling in her head;
A ghastly look she did assume;
She cries, "Alas, I am undone!"

"My loving father, you I leave;
For wicked Polly do not grieve;
For I must burn forevermore,
When thousand thousand years are o'er.

"Your councils I have slighted all,
My carnal appetite to fill.
When I am dead, remember well
Your wicked Polly groans in hell!"

She (w)rung her hands and groaned and cried,
And gnawed her tongue before she died,
Her nails turned black, her voice did fail,
She died and left this lower vale.

48

(A) JOHNNY SANDS

A man whose name was Johnny Sands
    Had married Betty Hague,
And though she brought him gold and lands,
    She proved a terrible plague.
For O she was a scolding wife,
    Full of caprice and whim,
He said that he was tired of life,
    And she was tired of him,
    And she was tired of him.

Says he, "Then I will drown myself,
    The river runs below."
Says she, "Pray do, you silly elf,
    I wished it long ago."
Says he, "Upon the brink I'll stand,
    Do you run down the hill
And push me in with all your might."
    Says she, "My love, I will."
    Says she, "My love, I will."

"For fear that I should courage lack
  And try to save myself,
Pray tie my hands behind my back."
  "I will," replied his wife.
She tied them fast, as you may think,
  And when securely done,
"Now stand," says she, "upon the brink,
  And I'll prepare to run,
  And I'll prepare to run."

And down the hill his loving bride
  Now ran with all her force
To push him in—he stepped aside
  And she fell in of course.
Now splashing, dashing, like a fish,
  "O save me, Johnny Sands."
"I can't, my dear, though much I wish,
  For you have tied my hands,
  For you have tied my hands."

(B) JOHNNY SANDS

A man whose name was Johnny Sands
  Had married Betty Hodge,
And though she brought him gold and land,
  She proved a terrible pledge,
For O she was a scolding wife,
  And full of whines and whims.
He said that he was tired of life
  And she was tired of him.

Says he, "Then I will drown myself
  In the river that runs below."
Says she, "Pray do, you silly elf,
  I wished it long ago."
"For fear that I should courage lack
  And try to save my life,
Pray tie my hands behind my back."
  "I will," replied his wife."

And now he's standing on the bank,
  She ran with all her force
To push him in—he stepped aside
  And she fell in of course.
Now splashing, dashing like a fish,
  "O, save me, Johnny Sands."
"I can't my dear, though much I wish,
  For you have tied my hands."

49

FULLER AND WARREN

Come ye sons of Columbia, your attention I do crave,
Whilst a sorrowful duty I will tell
That happened us of late, in our Indiana state,
Of a hero that none could excel·
Like Sampson he courted the choice of his life
And fully intended to make her his wife;
The golden ring he gave her was an emblem of true love,
And 'twas carved with the image of a dove.

This young couple they agreed to be married in speed;
This they vowed by the powers above.
But this fickle minded maid did again agree to wed
With young Warren, a liver in that place.
When Fuller came to know he was deprived of his love,
With a heart full of woe, unto Warren he did go,
Saying, "Warren, you have injured me to gratify your
    cause
By reporting that I left a prudent wife,
Now acknowledge that you've wronged me, or I will
    break the law,
Warren, I will rob you of your life."

Then Warren said to Fuller, "Sir, your question I deny,
And my heart to your true love it is bound;
And unto you I say, this is my wedding day,
In spite of all the heroes in the town."
Then Fuller in a passion of love and anger bound
Which at length caused many for to sigh,
For with one fatal shot he killed Warren on the spot,
And smiled as he said, "I am ready now to die."

Then Fuller was condemned by the honorable court,
And in Warrensburg was sentenced for to die
The ignominious death to hang above the earth
Like Haman on the gallows so high.
The day did arrive, young Fuller was to die,
Like an angel he did stand for he was a handsome man,
On his breast he wore the red, white and blue.

Ten thousand spectators were smote upon that spot
Whilst the guards dropped a tear from their eyes,
Saying, "Cursed is the *she* that caused this misery,
She herself instead of him had ought to die."
Now here's to all those who have been kind to loving
     wives,
You should crown them with honors and with light,
For marriage is a lottery and 'tis few that win the prize,
So, gentlemen, excuse me, goodnight!

50

POOR GOINS

Come all of you young people who lives far and near,
I'll tell you of a murder done on the Black Spur.

They surrounded poor Goins, but Goins got away;
He went to Eli Boggs' and there he did stay.

Old Eli's son Hughie his life did betray
By telling him he'd go with him to show him the way.

They took up the nine miles spar boys, they made no
    delay,
Afraid they would miss him and Goins get away.

When they saw him coming, they lay very still,
Saying, "It's money we're after, and Goins we'll kill."

They fired on poor Goins, which made his horse run;
The shot failed to kill him; George struck him with a
　　gun.

"Sweet heavens, sweet heavens!" poor Goins did cry,
"To think of my poor companion, and now I must die."

And when they had killed him, with him they would not
　　stay;
They then took his money and then rode away.

I wish you could have been there to hear her poor moan:
"Here lies his poor body, but where is his poor soul?"

51

POOR OMIE

"You promised to meet me at Adam's spring;
Some money you would bring me, or some other fine
　　thing."

"No money, no money, to flatter the case,
We'll go and get married, it will be no disgrace.

"Come jump up behind me and away we will ride
To yonder fair city; I will make you my bride."

She jumped up behind him and away they did go
To the banks of deep waters where they never overflow.

"O Omie, O Omie, I will tell you my mind;
My mind is to drown you and leave you behind."

"O pity! O pity! Pray spare me my life,
And I will deny you and not be your wife."

"No pity, no pity, no pity have I;
In yonder deep water your body shall lie."

He kicked her and stomped her, he threw her in the
   deep;
He jumped on his pony and rode at full speed.

The screams of poor Omie followed after him so nigh,
Saying, "I am a poor rebel not fitten to die."

She was missing one evening, next morning was found
In the bottom of Siloty below the mill dam.

Up stepped old Miss Mother, these words she did say,
"James Luther has killed Omie and he has run away.

"He has gone to Elk River, so I understand,
They have got him in prison for killing a man.

"They have got him in Ireland, bound down to the
   ground;
And he wrote a confession and sent it around.

" 'Go hang me or kill me, for I am the man
That drowned little Omie below the mill dam.' "

52

(A) SILVER DAGGER

Come all young men, please lend attention
  To these few words I'm going to write;
They are as true as ever were written
  Concerning a lady fair and bright.

A young man courted a fair young maiden;
  He loved her as he loved his life,
And always vowed that he would make her
  His own true and wedded wife.

But when his parents came to know this,
  They tried to part them day and night,
Saying, "Son, O son, don't you be so foolish—
  That girl's too poor for to be your wife."

This young man fell down on his knees a-pleading,
  "O father, mother, pity me.
Don't take from me my dearest darling,
  For she is all the world to me."

But when the young lady came to know this,
  She soon resolved what she would do.
She wandered forth and from the city,
  Never more her charms to view.

She wandered down by a bright flowing river,
    And sat herself beneath a tree.
She sighed and said, "O will I ever,
    Will I e'er more my true love see?"

Then up she picked her silver dagger,
    And pressed it through her snowy white breast.
She first did reel and then did stagger,
    Saying, "My true love, you come too late."

This young man being by the roadside heard her;
    He thought he knew his true love's voice.
He ran, he ran, like one distracted,
    Saying, "My true love, I fear you're lost."

He ran up to this dying body,
    Rolled it over into his arms,
Saying, "Neither gold nor friends can save you,
    For you are dying in my arms."

Her two pretty eyes like stars she opened,
    Saying, "My true love, you come too late.
Prepare to meet me on Mount Zion,
    Where all lover's joys shall be complete."

Then up he picked this bloody dagger,
    Pressed it through his aching heart;
And now, dear friends, may this be a warning
    To all who try to part true love.

(B) SILVER DAGGER

Come sit you down and give attention
   Of these few lines I am going to write.
'Tis of a comely youth whose name I'll mention
   Who lately courted a beauteous bride.

But when her parents came to know it,
   They strove, they strove, by night and day
To keep her from her own dear William.
   "He is poor," they would ofttimes say.

She being young and tender hearted,
   Not knowing what she must undergo,
She wandered far, she left the city,
   Some shady grove and field to view.

She being alone down by the river,
   All in the shade of a blooming tree,
She says, "And shall I, shall I ever,
   The wife of my Sweet William be?"

She then pulled out a silver dagger,
   And pierced it through her snowy white breast,
Saying these words, just as she staggered,
   "Farewell, true love, I'm going to rest."

He being lone down in the city,
   Hearing the moans this young lady made,

He run like one almost distracted,
   Saying, "Alas, I am undone."

She opened her eyes like stars a-drooping;
   She says, "True love, you have come too late.
Prepare to meet me on Mount Zion,
   Where all our joys will be complete."

He then picked up the silver dagger,
   And pierced it through his tender heart,
Saying, "Let this be an awful warning
   To all that do true lovers part."

53

THE AGED INDIAN

A hunter once built him a cabin
   In the depth of a forest wild,
And there in the lonely cabin
   He dwelt with his wife and child.

The smoke from the nearest wigwam
   Came curling over the hill,
It was built from the skins of the panther
   Which gave proof of the hunter's skill.

The hunter one early morning
   To a distant town had gone
Leaving his wife and Ida
   At home in the woods alone.

Ida's long brown lashes
   Hung over her eyes like silk,
As sitting down by the window
   She drank her basin of milk.

Suddenly a long dark shadow
   Came in at the open door
Shutting out all the sunlight
   Which fell across the floor.

As he stood in the open doorway
   The mother too well knew his will
Was to take her darling Ida
   To his wigwam over the hill.

He spoke with many a gesture.
   The mother was almost wild,
When she saw the aged Indian
   Departing with her child.

He carried her to his wigwam
   That stood just over the hill
And there with the aged Indian
   Forever she did dwell.

She taught him to read the Bible,
   And pray to the God that is true;
He taught her to tie and weave baskets
   Of a gold and azure hue.

54

CALOMEL

Ye doctors all of every rank
With their long bills that break a bank,
Of wisdom's learning, art, and skill
Seems all composed of calomel.

Since calomel has been their toast,
How many patients have they lost,
How many hundreds have they killed,
Or poisoned with their calomel.

If any fatal wretch be sick
Go call the doctor, haste, be quick,
The doctor comes with drop and pill,
But don't forget his calomel.

He enters, by the bed he stands,
He takes the patient by the hand,
Looks wise, sits down his pulse to feel,
And then takes out his calomel.

Next, turning to the patient's wife,
He calls for paper and a knife.
"I think your husband would do well
To take a dose of calomel."

The man grows worse, grows bad indeed
"Go call the doctor, ride with speed."

The doctor comes, the wife to tell
To double the dose of calomel.

The man begins in death to groan,
The fatal job for him is done,
The soul must go to heaven or hell,
A sacrifice to calomel.

The doctors of the present day
Mind not what an old woman say,
Nor do they mind me when I tell
I am no friend to calomel.

Well, if I must resign my breath,
Pray let me die a natural death,
And if I must bid all farewell,
Don't hurry me with calomel.

55

THE CREOLE GIRL

Over swamps and alligators I'm on my weary way
Over railroad ties and crossings, my weary feet did
stray,
Until the shades of evening some higher ground I
gained.
'Twas there I met a creole girl on the lakes of Pon-
chartrain.

"Good eve to you, fair maiden, my money does me no
    good;
If it were not for the alligators I would stay out in the
    wood."
"O welcome, welcome, stranger, although our house is
    plain;
We never turn a stranger out on the lakes of Ponchar-
    train."

She took me to her mother's house and treated me
    quite well,
Her hair in flowing ringlets around her shoulders fell.
I tried to paint her beauty, but I found it was in vain,
So beautiful was the creole girl on the lakes of Pon-
    chartrain.

I asked her if she would marry me, she said that never
    could be,
She said she had a lover, and he was far at sea.
She said she had a lover and true she would remain,
Till he came back to her again on the lakes of Pon-
    chartrain.

"Adieu, adieu, fair maiden, I never will see you more,
I'll never forget your kindness in the cottage by the
    shore.
At home in social circles, our flaming bowls we'll drain,
We'll drink to the health of the creole girl on the lakes
    of Ponchartrain."

56

THE BLUE AND THE GRAY

A mother's gift to her country's cause is a story yet
untold,
She had three sons, three only sons, each worth his
weight in gold.
She gave them up for the sake of war, while her heart
was filled with pain.
As each went away she was heard to say, "He will
never return again."

One lies down near Appomattox, many miles
away,
Another sleeps at Chickamauga, and they both
wore suits of gray.
'Mid the strains of "Down in Dixie" the third
was laid away,
In a trench at Santiago, the blue and the gray.

She's alone tonight, while the stars shine bright, with
a heart full of despair.
On the last great day I can hear her say, "My three
boys will be there.
Perhaps they'll watch at the heavenly gates, on guard
beside their guns.
Then the mother, true to the gray and blue, may enter
with her sons."

57

THE GAMBLER

My father was a gambler, he learnt me how to play,
My father was a gambler, he learnt me how to play,
Saying, "Son, don't go a-begging when you hold the
    ace and tray,
  When you hold the ace and tray."

    Hang me, O hang me, and I'll be dead and gone,
    Hang me, O hang me, and I'll be dead and gone,
    I wouldn't mind the hangin', it's bein' gone so
        long,
      It's layin' in my grave so long.

They took me down to old Fort Smith as sick as I
    could be,
They took me down to old Fort Smith as sick as I
    could be,
They handed me a letter saying, "Son, come home to
    me,"
  Saying, "Son, come home to me."

My father and my mother and my little sister makes
    three,
My father and my mother and my little sister makes
    three,
They all came up to the gallows to see the last of me.
  To see the last of me.

They put the rope around my neck and drew me very
    high,
They put the rope around my neck and drew me very
    high,
And the words I heard sayin' was, "It won't be long
    till he'll die,
  It won't be long till he'll die."

58

THE BAGGAGE COACH AHEAD

On a dark and stormy night as the train rolled on
    All passengers gone to bed,
Except a young man with a babe on his arm
    Sat sadly with bowed down head;
Just then the babe commenced crying
    As though its poor heart would break.
One angry man said, "Make that child stop its
    noise,
    For it's keeping us all awake."
"Put it out," said another, "Don't keep it in here;
    We've paid for our berth and want rest."
But never a word said the man with the child,
    As he fondled it close to his breast.
"O where is its mother?   Go take it to her,"
    One lady then softly said.
"I wish that I could," was the man's sad reply.
    "But she's dead in the coach ahead."

As the train rolled inward, a husband sat in
tears,
Thinking of the happiness of just a few
short years.
Baby's face brings pictures of a cherished
hope now dead,
But baby's cries can't awaken her in the
baggage coach ahead.

Every eye filled with tears as the story he told
Of a wife who was faithful and true;
He told how he'd saved up his earnings for years,
Just to build a home for two;
How when heaven had sent them their sweet little
babe,
Their young happy lives were blest;
His heart seemed to break when he mentioned her
name,
And in tears tried to tell them the rest.
Every woman arose to assist with the child;
There were mothers and wives on that train.
And soon was the little one sleeping in peace,
With no thought of sorrow or pain.
Next morn at the station he bade all goodbye,
"God bless you," he softly said,
Each one had a story to tell in their homes
Of the baggage coach ahead.

59

CASEY JONES

Come all you rounders for I want you to hear
The story told of an engineer;
Casey Jones was the rounder's name,
A heavy right (eight?) wheeler of a mighty fame.

Caller called Jones about half past four,
He kissed his wife at the station door,
Climbed into the cab with the orders in his hand,
Says, "This is my trip to the holy land."

Through South Memphis yards on the fly,
He heard the fore boy say, "You've got a white eye."
All the switchmen knew by the engine moan
That the man at the throttle was Casey Jones.

It had been raining some five or six weeks,
The railroad track was like the bed of a creek.
They rated him down to a thirty mile gait,
Threw the south-bound mail about eight hours late.

Foreman says, "Casey, you're runnin' too fast,
You run the block board the last station you passed."
Jones says, "Yes, I believe we'll make it, though,
For she steams better than I ever know."

Jones says, "Foreman, don't you fret;
Keep knockin' at the fire door, don't give up yet

I'm going to run her till she leaves the rail,
Or make it on time with the Southern mail."

Around the curve and down the dump,
Two locomotives were bound to bump.
Foreman hollered, "Jones, it's just ahead,
We might jump and make it, but we'll all be dead."

'Twas around this curve he spied a passenger train,
Rousing his engine he caused the bell to ring;
Foreman jumped off, but Jones stayed on—
He's a good engineer, but he's dead and gone.

Poor Casey Jones was all right,
For he stuck to his duty both day and night,
They loved to hear his whistle and ring of number
    three,
As he came into Memphis on the old I. C.

Headaches and heartaches and all kinds of pain
Are not apart from a railroad train;
Tales that are in earnest, noble, and grand,
Belong to the life of a railroad man.

60

THE LADY ELGIN

Up from the man's cottage,
    Forth from the mansion door,

Sweeping across the waters
  And echoing to the shore,
Caught by the morning breezes,
  Borne on the evening gale,
Cometh a voice of mourning,
  A sad and solemn wail.

        Lost on the Lady Elgin,
        Sleeping to wake no more,
        Numbered in death three hundred
        Who failed to reach the shore.

O it's the cry of children
  Weeping for parents gone,
Children who slept at evening
  But orphans awoke at dawn;
Sisters for brother weeping,
  Husbands for missing wives,
Such were the ties dissevered
  With those three hundred lives.

61

THE JAMESTOWN FLOOD

Is it news you ask for, strangers, as you stand and gaze
    around
At those cold and lifeless bodies lying here upon the
    ground?
Do you see that lady yonder, with the little girl and
    boy?

That's my wife, my darling Minnie, once my house-
hold pride and joy.

Just an hour ago I brought them from the river's fatal
tide,
Laid them here where now you see them, all together
side by side.
Strangers, if you'll turn to listen to my story long and
sad,
You'll confess it is no wonder that today I'm almost
mad.

We were seated at the table chatting in a happy mood,
When we heard a mighty rushing like some great and
awful flood,
Nearer! nearer! came the water, till at last it reached
our home,
O the horror of the moment when we realized our
doom!

Not one moment did we tarry, but with cheeks and
brow aglow
Climbed we to the topmost chamber for how long I do
not know,
Then I clasped my wife and children to my chilled and
aching heart
For I saw that soon or later we would surely have to
part.

Faster, faster rushed the waters; tighter, tighter grew
my grasp

Till a wave of mud and fury tore both children from
my clasp
Then my wife grew faint and trembly, cold and white
her marble brow,
One low whisper, scarcely spoken; "You are all that's
left me now.

"Let your arms enfold me, husband, lay your head
upon my breast,
O, our children, may he guide them to a place of peace
and rest;
May he spare you to me, darling, to protect"—But
while she spoke
Downward rushed a mighty current and my deathlike
grasp was broke.

Down she went, my last sweet darling, she my true and
loving wife,
She had been my joy and comfort all along the path of
life.
Just as in a dream I stood there till at last a shout
I heard,
From some men who stood above me, "Grasp the rope,
we'll help you out."

And before night's sable curtain spread across the
angry wave
I was drawn above and rescued from a cold and watery
grave,
But my darling wife and children floated on till one by one

They were found and carried to me, but their work on
    earth was done.

Sad and mournful as I stood there, saw no signs of life
    or breath;
O'er my heart fell deep dark shadows as I saw them
    cold in death.
And a flood of thought came o'er me, overwhelming
    mind and heart,
And my soul cried out within me, "O my loved ones,
    must we part?

Fare thee well, my wife and children, in my heart
    you'll ever be
Till I too shall cross the river where we will united be,
Then we'll have the joy of loving as we never loved
    before,
Where no hearts are chilled and broken, in the sweet
    forevermore."

62

THE MILWAUKEE FIRE

'Twas the gray of early morning when the dreadful cry
    of fire
Rang out upon the cold and piercing air;
Just that little word alone is all it would require
To spread dismay and panic everywhere.
Milwaukee was excited as it never was before,

On learning that the fire bells all around
Were ringing to eternity a hundred souls or more
And the Newhall house was burning to the ground.

> O hear the firebells ringing at the morning's
> early dawn.
> Hear the voices as they give that dreadful cry!
> O hear the wail of terror 'mid the fierce and
> burning flames.
> Heaven protect them for they're waiting there
> to die.

The firemen worked like demons and did all within
their power
To save a life or try to soothe a pain.
It made the strongest heart sick, for in less than half
an hour
All was hushed and further efforts were in vain.
When the dread alarm was sounded through the oft,
condemned hotel
They rushed in mad confusion every way.
The smoke was suffocating and blinding them as well;
The fire king could not be held at bay.

At every window men and women wildly would beseech
For help in tone of anguish and despair;
What must have been their feelings where the ladders
could not reach
As they felt death's grasp round them everywhere.
Up in the highest window stood a servant girl alone;

The crowd beneath all gazed with bated breath;
They turned away their faces; there was many a stifled
  groan
When she jumped to meet perhaps as hard a death.

A boy stood in a window and his mother was below;
She saw him, and the danger drawing near;
With hands upraised to pray for him she knelt down
  in the snow,
And the stoutest men could not restrain a tear.
She madly rushed toward the fire and wildly tore her
  hair
"Take me, O God, but spare my pride, my joy."
She saw the flames surround him and then in dark
  despair
Said, "God have mercy on my only son."

63

THE FATAL WEDDING

The wedding bells were ringing
  On a moonlight winter's night;
The church was decorated,
  All within was gay and bright.
A mother with her baby
  Came and saw the light aglow.
She thought of how those same bells chimed
  For her three years ago.

While the wedding bells were ringing
  And the bride and groom were there,
Marching up the aisle together
  While the organ pealed an air,
Speaking words of fond affection,
  Vowing never more to part,
Just another fatal wedding,
  Just another broken heart.

"I'd like to be admitted, sir,
  She told the sexton old,
Just for the sake of baby,
  To protect him from the cold."
He told her that the wedding
  Was for the rich and grand,
And with the eager watching crowd
  Outside she'd have to stand.

She begged the sexton once again
  To let her step inside,
"For baby's sake you may come in,"
  The gray-haired man replied.
"If anyone knows reason why
  This couple should not wed
Speak now or hold your peace forever,"
  Soon the preacher said.

"I must object," the woman cried
  With voice so meek and mild,
"The bridegroom is my husband,
  And this our little child."

"What proof have you?" the preacher said,
    "My infant," she replied,
Then raised the babe and knelt to pray;
    The little one had died.

The parents of the bride then took
    The outcast by the hand,
"We'll care for you through life," they said,
    "You've saved our child from harm."
The outcast wife, the bride, and parents
    Then quickly drove away.
The husband died by his own hand
    Before the break of day.

No wedding feast that night was spread,
    Two graves were made next day,
One for the babe, and in the one
    The father soon was laid.
This story has been often told,
    By fireside warm and bright,
Of bride and groom and outcast
    On that fatal wedding night.

SONGS OF CRIMINALS
AND OUTLAWS

64

(A)   JESSE JAMES

How the people held their breath
When they heard of Jesse's death,
  And wondered how he came to die;
For the big reward little Robert Ford
  Shot Jesse James on the sly.

  Jesse leaves a widow to mourn all her life,
    The children he left will pray
  For the thief and the coward
    Who shot Mr. Howard
  And laid Jesse James in his grave.

Jesse was a man,
A friend to the poor,
  Never did he suffer a man's pain;
And with his brother Frank
He robbed the Chicago bank,
  And stopped the Glendale train.

Jesse goes to rest
With his hand on his breast,
  And the devil will be upon his knees;
He was born one day in the county of Clay,
  And came from a great race.

Men when you go out to the West,
  Don't be afraid to die;

With the law in their hand,
But they didn't have the sand
 For to take Jesse James alive.

(B) JESSE JAMES

Jesse James was a man, and he had a robber band;
And he flagged down the eastern bound train.
Robert Ford watched his eye,
And he shot him on the sly,
And they laid Jesse James in his grave.

 Poor old Jesse, poor old Jesse James,
 And they laid Jesse James in his grave.
 Robert Ford's pistol ball,
 Brought him tumbling from the wall,
 And they laid Jesse James in his grave.

Jesse James' little wife
Was a moaner all her life,
When they laid Jesse James in his grave.
She earned her daily bread
By her needle and her thread,
When they laid Jesse James in his grave.

65

(A) CHARLES GUITEAU
or
JAMES A. GARFIELD

Come all you tender Christians,
Wherever you may be,

And likewise pay attention
To these few lines from me.
For the murder of James A. Garfield
I am condemned to die,
On the thirtieth day of June
Upon the scaffold high.

My name is Charles Guiteau,
My name I'll ne'er deny.
I leave my aged parents
In sorrow for to die.
But little did they think,
While in my youthful bloom,
I'd be taken to the scaffold
To meet my earthly doom.

'Twas down at the station
I tried to make my escape,
But Providence being against me
There proved to be no show.
They took me off to prison
While in my youthful bloom
To be taken to the scaffold
To meet my earthly doom.

I tried to be insane
But I found it ne'er would do,
The people were all against me,
To escape there was no clue.
Judge Cox, he read my sentence,

His clerk he wrote it down,
I'd be taken to the scaffold
To meet my earthly doom.

My sister came to see me,
To bid a last farewell.
She threw her arm around me
And wept most bitterly.
She says, "My darling brother,
This day you must cruelly die
For the murder of James A. Garfield
Upon the scaffold high."

(B) THE DEATH OF BENDALL

Come all ye tender Christians and hearken unto me,
And kindly pay attention to these few words from me.
For the murder of young Bendall I am condemned to
die;
On the fourteenth of November I mount the gallows
high.

My name is J. S. Birchell, my name I'll never
deny.
I leave my aged parents in sorrow for to die;
It's little did I think when in my childhood home,
I'd be taken to the scaffold to meet my fatal
doom.

Now Bendall he was young and in the prime of life,
To come out here to Canada to lead an honest life;
But Birchell he betrayed him, he led him to the swamp,
And there he drew his pistol and Bendall he did drop.

My wife she came to see me, to bid her last farewell.
She threw her arms around me and wept most bitterly;
Said she, "My darling husband, tomorrow you must die
For the murder of young Bendall you mount the scaf-
    fold high."

He tried to play off innocent, but he found it was no go.
The people turned against him and proved to give no
    show.
And when those words were spoken, those words "Thy
    will be done,"
The trap door, it was opened, and Birchell he was hung.

66

SAM BASS ©

Sam Bass was born in Indiana, it was his native home,
And at the age of seventeen young Sam began to roam.
Sam first came out to Texas a cowboy for to be,—
A kinder-hearted fellow you seldom ever see.

Sam used to deal in race stock, one called the Denton
    mare,
He matched her in scrub races, and took her to the
    fair.

Sam used to coin the money and spent it just as
    free,
He always drank good whiskey wherever he might be.

Sam left the Collins ranch in the merry month of May
With a herd of Texas cattle the Black Hills for to see,
Sold out in Custer City and then got on a spree,—
A harder set of cowboys you seldom ever see.

On their way back to Texas they robbed the U. P.
    train,
And then split up in couples and started out again.
Joe Collins and his partner were overtaken soon,
With all their hard-earned money they had to meet
    their doom.

Sam made it back to Texas all right side up with care;
Rode into the town of Denton with all his friends to
    share.
Sam's life was short in Texas; three robberies did he do,
He robbed all the passenger, mail, and express cars too.

Sam had four companions—four bold and daring lads—
They were Richardson, Jackson, Joe Collins, and Old
    Dad;
Four more bold and daring cowboys the rangers never
    knew,
They whipped the Texas rangers and ran the boys in
    blue.

Sam had another companion, called Arkansas for
    short,
Was shot by a Texas ranger by the name of Thomas
    Floyd;
O, Tom is a big six-footer and thinks he's mighty fly,
But I can tell you his racket,—he's a deadbeat on the
    sly.

Jim Murphy was arrested, and then released on bail;
He jumped his bond at Tyler and then took the train
    for Terrell;
But Mayor Jones had posted Jim and that was all a
    stall,
'Twas only a plan to capture Sam before the coming
    of fall.

Sam met his fate at Round Rock, July the twenty-
    first,
They pierced poor Sam with rifle balls and emptied out
    his purse.
Poor Sam he is a corpse and six foot under clay,
And Jackson's in the bushes trying to get away.

Jim had borrowed Sam's good gold and didn't want to
    pay,
The only shot he saw was to give poor Sam away.
He sold out Sam and Barnes and left their friends to
    mourn,—
O what a scorching Jim will get when Gabriel blows
    his horn.

And so he sold out Sam and Barnes and left their
    friends to mourn,
O what a scorching Jim will get when Gabriel blows
    his horn.
Perhaps he's got to heaven, there's none of us can say,
But if I'm right in my surmise he's gone the other way.

67

JACK WILLIAMS

I am a boatman by trade,
    Jack Williams is my name,
And by a false deluding girl
    Was brought to grief and shame.

On Chatton street I did reside,
    Where the people did me know;
I fell in love with a pretty pretty girl,
    She proved my overthrow.

I took to robbing night and day,
    All to maintain her fine and gay.
What I got I valued not
    But I gave to her straightway.

At last to Newgate I was brought,
    Bound down in irons strong.
With rattling chains around my legs,
    She longed to see me hang.

I wrote a letter to my love
Some comfort for to find.
Instead of proving a friend to me
  She proved to me unkind.

And in a scornful manner said
  "I hate your company,
And as you have made your bed, young man,
  Down on it you may lie."

There is a heaven above us all
  And it proved kind to me;
I broke my chains and scaled the walls,
  And gained sweet liberty.

Now I am at liberty,
  A solemn vow I'll take;
I'll shun all evil company
  For that false woman's sake.

68

YOUNG McFEE

Come all my friends and listen to me,
While I relate a sad and mournful history.
On this day I'll tell to thee
The story of young McFee.

I scarce had reached to my fifth year
Before my father and mother dear
Both in their silent graves were laid
By He whom first their beings gave.
I took unto myself a wife.
She'd be living yet, there is no doubt,
If I had not met Miss Hattie Stout.
My wife was lying on the bed
When I approached her and said,
"Dear wife, here is some medicine I have brought,
That I for you this day have bought.
Pray take it, do, it will cure you
Of those vile fits.   Pray take it, do."
She gave to me one loving look
And in her mouth the poison took.
Down on her bed low with her babe,
Down to her last long sleep she laid.
I fearing that she was not dead
My hands upon her throat I laid,
And there such deep impression made
That her soul from sorrow quicker fled,
And my heart was filled with woe.
I cried, "O whither shall I go?
How can I leave this mournful place,
This world again how can I pace?

Had I ten thousand pounds, I'd give
To bring her back again to live,
To bring her back again to life,
My dear, my darling murdered wife."

69

MY BONNY BLACK BESS

Let the lover his mistress's beauty rehearse,
And laud her attractions in languishing verse;
Be it mine in rude strain but with truth to express
The love that I bear to my Bonny Black Bess.

From the West was her dam, from the East was her
    sire;
From the one came her swiftness, the other her fire;
No peer of the realm better blood can possess
Than flows in the blood of my Bonny Black Bess.

Look! Look! how that eyeball glows bright as a brand,
That neck proudly arching, those nostrils expand;
Mark that wide flowing mane, of which each silky tress
Might adorn prouder beauties, though none like Black
    Bess.

Mark that skin sleek as velvet and dusky as night,
With its jet undisfigured by one lock of white,
That throat branched with veins, prompt to charge or
    caress,
Now is she not beautiful, bonny Black Bess?

Over highway and byway, in rough or smooth weather,
Some thousands of miles have we journeyed together;

Our couch the same straw, our meals the same mess,
No couple more constant than I and Black Bess.

By moonlight, in darkness, by night and by day
Her headlong career there is nothing can stay;
She cares not for distance, she knows not distress.
Can you show me a courser to match with Black Bess?

Once it happened in Cheshire, near Durham, I popped
On a horseman alone whom I suddenly stopped;
That I lightened his pockets you'll readily guess—
Quick work makes Dick Turpin when mounted on
    Bess.

Now it seems the man knew me: "Dick Turpin," said
    he,
"You shall swing for this job, as you live, d'ye see?"
I laughed at his threats and his vows of redress—
I was sure of an alibi then with Black Bess.

Brake, brook, meadow, and ploughed field Bess fleetly
    bestrode;
As the crow wings his flight we selected our road.
We arrived at Hough Green in five minutes or less,
My neck it was saved by the speed of Black Bess.

Stepping carelessly forward I lounge on the green,
Taking excellent care that by all I am seen;
Some remarks on time's flight to the squires I address;
But I say not a word of the flight of Black Bess.

I mention the hour—it is just about four,
Play a rubber at bowls, think the danger is o'er,
When athwart my next game like a checkmate in chess
Comes the horseman in search of the rider of Bess.

What matter details?   Off with triumph I came.
He swears to the hour and the squires swear the same.
I had robbed him at four, while at four, they profess
I was quietly bowling—all thanks to Black Bess.

Then one halloo, boys, one loud cheering halloo,
For the swiftest of coursers, the gallant, the true,
For the sportsman inborn shall the memory bless
Of the horse of the highwaymen, Bonny Black Bess.

70

TURPIN AND THE LAWYER

As Turpin was riding across a moor,
There he saw a lawyer riding on before.
Turpin riding up to him, said, "Are you not afraid
To meet Dick Turpin, that mischievous blade?"

Singing Eh ro, Turpin I ro.

Says Turpin to the lawyer for to be cute,
"I hid my money into my boot."
Says the lawyer to Turpin, "He can't find mine,
For I hid it in the cape of my coat behind."

They rode along together to the foot of the hill,
When Turpin bid the lawyer to stand still,
Saying, "The cape of your coat it must come off,
For my horse is in want of a new saddle-cloth."

Turpin robbed the lawyer of all his store,
He told him to go home and he would get more,
"And the very first town that you come in,
You can tell them you was robbed by Dick
    Turpin."

71

JACK DONAHOO ©

Come all you bold undaunted men, you outlaws of
    the day,
It's time to beware of the ball and chain and also
    slavery.
Attention pay to what I say, and verily if you do,
I will relate you the actual fate of bold Jack Donahoo.

He had scarcely landed as I tell you, upon Australia's
    shore,
Than he became a real highwayman, as he had been
    before.
There was Underwood and Mackerman, and Wade
    and Westley too,
These were the four associates of bold Jack Donahoo.

Jack Donahoo who was so brave, rode out that after-
    noon,
Knowing not that the pain of death would overtake
    him soon.
So quickly then the horse police from Sidney came
    to view;
"Begone from here, you cowardly dogs," says bold
    Jack Donahoo.

The captain and the sergeant stopped then to decide.
"Do you intend to fight us or unto us resign?"
"To surrender to such cowardly dogs is more than
    I will do,
This day I'll fight if I lose my life," says bold Jack
    Donahoo.

The captain and the sergeant the men they did divide;
They fired from behind him and also from each side;
It's six police he did shoot down before the fatal ball
Did pierce the heart of Donahoo and cause bold Jack
    to fall.

And when he fell he closed his eyes, he bid the world
    adieu;
Come, all you boys, and sing the song of bold Jack
    Donahoo.

72

CAPTAIN KIDD

"My parents taught me well, as I sailed, as I sailed,
To shun the gates of hell as I sailed.
I cursed my father dear, and her that did me bear,
And so wickedly did swear, as I sailed, as I sailed,
  And so wickedly did swear, as I sailed.

"I'd a Bible in my hand, when I sailed, when I sailed,
But I sunk it in the sand as I sailed.
I made a solemn vow, to God I would not bow,
Nor myself one prayer allow, when I sailed, when I
  sailed,
  Nor myself one prayer allow, when I sailed.

"I murdered William Moore as I sailed, as I sailed,
And left him in his gore as I sailed,
And being cruel still, my gunner did I kill,
And much precious blood did spill, as I sailed, as
  I sailed,
  And much precious blood did spill as I sailed.

"My name was Robert Kidd as I sailed, as I sailed,
My name was Robert Kidd, as I sailed.
My name was Robert Kidd, God's laws I did forbid,
And so wickedly I did, as I sailed, as I sailed,
  And so wickedly I did as I sailed!"

WESTERN BALLADS
AND SONGS

73

THE TEXAS RANGERS

Come all you Texas Rangers wherever you may be,
I'll tell you of some trouble which happened unto me.

My name 'tis nothing extra, the truth to you I'll tell,
Come all you jolly Rangers, I'm sure I wish you well.

It was the age of sixteen I joined the royal band,
We marched from San Antonio, unto the Rio Grande.

Our captain he informed us, perhaps he thought
 'twas right,
Before we reached the station, he was sure we would
 have to fight.

It was one morning early, our captain gave command,
"To arms, to arms," he shouted, "and by your horses
 stand."

We heard those Indians coming, we heard them give
 their yell,
My feelings at that moment no human tongue can tell.

We saw their smoke arising, it almost reached the
 sky,
My feelings at that moment, now is my time to die.

We saw those Indian's coming, their arrows around us
    hailed,
My heart it sank within me, my courage almost failed.

We fought them full nine hours until the strife was
    o'er,
The like of dead and wounded, I never saw before.

Five hundred as noble Rangers as ever served the west,
We'll bury those noble Rangers, sweet peace shall be
    their rest.

I thought of my poor mother, those words she said
    to me,
"To you they are all strangers, you had better stay
    with me."

I thought she was old and childish, perhaps she did
    not know,
My mind was bent on roving and I was bound to go.

Perhaps you have a mother, likewise a sister too,
Perhaps you have a sweetheart to weep and mourn
    for you.

If this be your condition I advise you to never roam,
I advise you by experience you had better stay at
    home.

74

THE LITTLE OLD SOD SHANTY ON THE CLAIM

I am looking rather seedy now,
While holding down my claim,
And my victuals are not always served the best;
And the mice play slyly round me,
As I nestle down to sleep
In my little old sod shanty in the West.

The hinges are of leather, and the windows have
      no glass
While the board roof lets the howling blizzard in,
And I hear the hungry coyote
As he sneaks up through the grass
Around the little old sod shanty on my claim.

Yet I rather like the novelty of living in this way,
Though my bill of fare is always rather tame,
But I'm as happy as a clam
On this land of Uncle Sam's,
In my little old sod shanty on my claim.

But when I left my Eastern home, a bachelor so gay,
To try to win my way to wealth and fame,
I little thought that I'd come down to burning twisted
      hay
In my little old sod shanty on my claim.

75

COWBOY SONG

One night as I lay on the prairie
    And looked at the stars in the sky,
I wondered if ever a cowboy
    Would drift to that sweet Bye and Bye.

The trail to that bright mystic region
    Is narrow and dim, so they say;
But the one that leads down to perdition
    Is staked and is blazed all the way.

They say that there'll be a great roundup,
    Where cowboys like "dogies" will stand,
Cast out by those riders from heaven
    Who are posted and know every brand.

I wonder, was there ever a cowboy
    Prepared for the great Judgment Day,
Who could say to the boss of the riders,
    "I'm ready to be driven away."

They say he will never forsake you,
    That he notes every action and look,
But for safety you'd better get branded
    And have your name in his great book.

For they tell of another great owner
  Who is nigh overstocked, so they say,
But who always makes room for the sinner
  Who strays from the bright narrow way.

76

THE OLD CHISHOLM TRAIL ©

Come along, boys, and listen to my tale,
I'll tell you of my troubles on the old Chisholm trail.

  Coma ti yi youpy, youpy ya, youpy ya,
  Coma ti yi youpy, youpy ya.

I started up the trail October twenty-third.
I started up the trail with the 2-U herd.

Oh, a ten dollar hoss and a forty dollar saddle,—
And I'm goin' to punchin' Texas cattle.

I woke up one morning on the old Chisholm trail,
Rope in my hand and a cow by the tail.

I'm up in the mornin' afore daylight
And afore I sleep the moon shines bright.

Old Ben Bolt was a blamed good boss,
But he'd go to see the girls on a sore-backed hoss.

Old Ben Bolt was a fine old man
And you'd know there was whiskey wherever he'd land.

My hoss throwed me off at the creek called Mud,
My hoss throwed me off round the 2-U herd.

Last time I saw him he was going cross the level
A-kicking up his heels and a-running like the devil.

It's cloudy in the West, a-looking like rain,
And my damned old slicker's in the wagon again.

Crippled my hoss, I don't know how,
Ropin' at the horns of a 2-U cow.

We hit Caldwell and we hit her on the fly,
We bedded down the cattle on the hill close by.

No chaps, no slicker, and it's pouring down rain,
And I swear by god, I'll never night-herd again.

Feet in the stirrups and seat in the saddle,
I hung and rattled with them long-horn cattle.

Last night I was on guard and the leader broke the
    ranks,
I hit my horse down the shoulders and I spurred him
    in the flanks.

The wind commenced to blow, and the rain began to
    fall,
Hit looked, by grab, like we was goin' to lose 'em all.

I jumped in the saddle and grabbed holt the horn,
Best blamed cow-puncher ever was born.

I popped my foot in the stirrup and gave a little yell,
The tail cattle broke and the leaders went to hell.

I don't give a damn if they never do stop;
I'll ride as long as an eight-day clock.

Foot in the stirrup and hand on the horn,
Best damned cowboy ever was born.

I herded and I hollered and I done very well,
Till the boss said, "Boys, just let 'em go to hell."

Stray in the herd and the boss said kill it,
So I shot him in the rump with the handle of the
    skillet.

We rounded 'em up and put 'em on the cars,
And that was the last of the old Two Bars.

Oh it's bacon and beans 'most every day,—
I'd as soon be a-eatin' prairie hay.

I'm on my best horse and I'm goin' at a run,
I'm the quickest shootin' cowboy that ever pulled a
  gun.

I went to the wagon to get my roll,
To come back to Texas, dad-burn my soul.

I went to my boss to draw my roll,
He had figgered it out I was nine dollars in the hole.

I'll sell my outfit just as soon as I can,
I won't punch cattle for no damned man.

Goin' back to town to draw my money,
Goin' back home to see my honey.

With my knees in the saddle and my seat in the sky,
I'll quit punching cows in the sweet by and by.

>   Coma ti yi youpy, youpy ya, youpy ya,
>   Coma ti yi youpy, youpy ya.

77

THE DYING COWBOY

As I walked through Tom Sherman's bar-room,
  Tom Sherman's bar-room on a bright summer's day,
There I spied a handsome young cowboy
  All dressed in white linen as though for the grave.

Beat your drums lowly, and play your fifes slowly,
   Play the dead march as you bear me along,
Take me to the graveyard and lay the sod o'er me,
   For I'm a dying cowboy and know I've done
      wrong.

"I know by your appearance you must be a cowboy,"
   These words he said as I came passing by,
"Come sit down beside me, and hear my sad story,
   I'm shot through the breast and know I must die.

"Once in my saddle I used to look handsome,
   Once in my saddle I used to feel gay,
I first went to drinking, then went to gambling,
   Got into a fight which ended my day.

"Go and tell my gray-haired mother,
   Break the news gently to sister dear,
But never a word of this place must you mention
   When a crowd gathers round you, my story to hear."

78

O BURY ME NOT ON THE LONE PRAIRIE

"O bury me not on the lone prairie,"
These words came slowly and mournfully
From the pallid lips of a youth who lay
On his cold damp bed at the close of day.

"O bury me not on the lone prairie
Where the wild coyote will howl o'er me,
Where the cold wind weeps and the grasses wave;
No sunbeams rest on a prairie grave."

He has wasted and pined till o'er his brow
Death's shades are slowly gathering now;
He thought of his home with his loved ones nigh,
As the cowboys gathered to see him die.

Again he listened to well known words,
To the wind's soft sigh and the song of birds;
He thought of his home and his native bowers,
Where he loved to roam in his childhood hours.

"I've ever wished that when I died,
My grave might be on the old hillside,
Let there the place of my last rest be—
O bury me not on the lone prairie!

"O'er my slumbers a mother's prayer
And a sister's tears will be mingled there;
For 'tis sad to know that the heart-throb's o'er,
And that its fountain will gush no more.

"In my dreams I say"— but his voice failed there;
And they gave no heed to his dying prayer;
In a narrow grave six feet by three,
They buried him there on the lone prairie.

May the light winged butterfly pause to rest
O'er him who sleeps on the prairie's crest;
May the Texas rose in the breezes wave
O'er him who sleeps in a prairie's grave.

And the cowboys now as they roam the plain,
(For they marked the spot where his bones have lain)
Fling a handful of roses over his grave,
With a prayer to him who his soul will save.

79

I WANT TO BE A COWBOY

I want to be a cowboy and with the cowboys stand,
Big spurs upon my bootheels and a lasso in my hand;
My hat broad brimmed and belted upon my head
    I'll place,
And wear my chaparajos with elegance and grace.

The first bright beam of sunlight that paints the east
    with red
Would call me forth to breakfast on bacon, beans,
    and bread;
And then upon my broncho so festive and so bold
I'd rope the frisky heifer and chase the three year old.

And when my work is over to Cheyenne then I'll head,
Fill up on beer and whiskey and paint the damn town
    red.

I'll gallop through the front streets with many a
frightfull yell;
I'll rope the slant old heathen and yank them straight
to hell.

80

WHOOPEE TI YI YO, GIT ALONG LITTLE
DOGIES ©

As I walked out one morning for pleasure,
I spied a cow-puncher all riding alone;
His hat was throwed back and his spurs was a-jingling,
As he approached me a-singin' this song.

    Whoopee ti yi yo, git along little dogies,
    It's your misfortune, and none of my own,
    Whoopee ti yi yo, git along little dogies,
    For you know Wyoming will be your new home.

Early in the spring we round up the dogies,
Mark and brand and bob off their tails;
Round up our horses, load up the chuck-wagon,
Then throw the dogies upon the trail.

It's whooping and yelling and driving the dogies;
Oh, how I wish you would go on;
It's whooping and punching and go on little dogies,
For you know Wyoming will be your new home.

Some boys goes up the trail for pleasure,
But that's where you get it most awfully wrong;
For you haven't any idea the trouble they gave us
While we go driving them along.

When the night comes on and we hold them on the
    bedground,
These little dogies that roll on so slow;
Roll up the herd and cut out the strays,
And roll the little dogies that never rolled before.

Your mother she was raised way down in Texas,
Where the jimson weed and sand-burrs grow;
Now we'll fill you up on prickly pear and cholla
Till you are ready for the trail to Idaho.

Oh you'll be soup for Uncle Sam's Injuns;
"It's beef, heap beef," I hear them cry.
Git along, git along, git along little dogies,
You're going to be beef steers by and by.

81

CHEYENNE BOYS

Come all you pretty girls and listen to my noise,
I'll tell you not to marry the Cheyenne boys,
For if you do a portion it will be;
Cold butter milk and Johnnie cake is all you'll see.
Cold butter milk and Johnnie cake is all you'll see.

They'll take you down to a sandy hill,
Take you down contrary to your will;
Put you down in some lonesome place,
And that's just the way with the Cheyenne race,
And that's just the way with the Cheyenne race.

When they go to church I'll tell you what they wear,
An old gray coat all covered with hair,
An old gray coat all torn down,
A stove-pipe hat more rim than crown,
A stove-pipe hat more rim than crown.

When they go in, down they set,
Take out their handerchief and wipe off the sweat,
Look at all the pretty girls and then begin to laugh,
And roll around their eyes like a dying calf,
And roll around their eyes like a dying calf.

82

BREAKING IN A TENDERFOOT

'Twas then I thought I'd have some fun,
And see how cowpunching was done;
So when the roundups had begun
I tackled a cattle king.

Says he, "My foreman's here in town;
He stops at Dyer's, his name's Brown."
We started for the ranch next day;

The foreman jollied me all the way,
"Cowpunching was only play."

"'Twas just like drifting with the tide,"
All I'd have to do was to ride;
But that old sinner, how he lied,
O didn't he have his gall!

They saddled me up on an old gray hack,
With a great big "set-fast" on his back,
And padded him up with a gunny sack,
They used my bedding all.

First he was up and then he was down,
Jumped up in the air and turned around,
And when at last I hit the ground,
I had an awful fall.

They picked me up and carried me in,
And rubbed me down with a rolling pin,
"That's the way we all begin,
You've done well," says Brown.

"If by tomorrow you don't die,
We'll give you another horse to try."
"O won't you let me walk?" says I.
Says Brown, "Yes, into town."

They gave me charge of the cavvy herd,
And told me not to work too hard,

That all I had to do was guard,
Those cattle from gettin' away.

I had three hundred and sixty head,
And I sometimes wished that I was dead;
Sometimes my horse would fall,
And I'd go on like a cannon ball.

So before you go cowpunching,
Kiss your wife,
Get a heavy insurance on your life,
Then cut your throat with a carving knife,
This is the only way.

83

STARVING TO DEATH ON A GOVERNMENT CLAIM

Frank Baker's my name, and a bachelor I am.
I'm keeping old batch on an elegant plan,
You'll find me out west in the county of Lane,
A-starving to death on a government claim.

My house is constructed of natural soil,
The walls are erected according to Hoyle,
The roof has no pitch, but is level and plain,
And I never get wet till it happens to rain.

Hurrah for Lane county, the land of the free,
The home of the grasshopper, bed-bug, and flea,

I'll holler its praises, and sing of its fame,
While starving to death on a government claim.

How happy I am as I crawl into bed,
The rattlesnakes rattling a tune at my head,
While the gay little centipede, so void of all fear,
Crawls over my neck, and into my ear;
And the gay little bed-bug so cheerful and bright,
He keeps me a-going two-thirds of the night.

My clothes are all ragged, my language is rough,
My bread is case-hardened, both solid and tough,
The dough it is scattered all over the room,
And the floor would get scared at the sight of a broom.

The dishes are scattered all over the bed,
All covered with sorghum, and government bread,
Still I have a good time, and I live at my ease,
On common sop sorghum, an' bacon an' cheese.

How happy I am on my government claim,
I've nothing to lose, I've nothing to gain,
I've nothing to eat and I've nothing to wear,
And nothing from nothing is honest and fair.

Oh, here I am safe, so here I will stay,
My money's all gone, and I can't get away,
There's nothing to make a man hard and profane,
Like starving to death on a government claim.

Now come on to Lane county, there's room for you all,
Where the wind never ceases, and the rains never fall,
Come join in our chorus to sing for its fame,
You sinners that're stuck on your government claim.

Now hurrah for Lane county, where the blizzards arise,
The wind never ceases, and the moon never rise,
Where the sun never sets, but it always remains,
Till it burns us all out on our government claims.

Now don't get discouraged, you poor hungry men.
You're all just as free as the pig in the pen,
Just stick to your homestead, and battle the fleas,
And look to your Maker to send you a breeze.

Hurrah for Lane county, the land of the West,
Where the farmers and laborers are ever at rest;
There's nothing to do but to stick and remain,
And starve like a dog on a government claim.

Now, all your poor sinners, I hope you will stay,
And chew the hard rag till you're toothless and gray,
But as for myself, I'll no longer remain,
To starve like a dog on a government claim.

Farewell to Lane county, farewell to the West,
I'll travel back east to the girl I love best,
I'll stop at Missouri and get me a wife,
Then live on corn dodgers, the rest of my life.

84

THE BUFFALO SKINNERS ©

Come all you jolly fellows and listen to my song,
There are not many verses, it will not detain you long;
It's concerning some young fellows who did agree to go
And spend one summer pleasantly on the range of the
buffalo.

It happened in Jacksboro in the spring of seventy-three,
A man by the name of Crego came stepping up to me,
Saying, "How do you do, young fellow, and how would
you like to go
And spend one summer pleasantly on the range of the
buffalo?"

It's me being out of employment, this to Crego I did
say,
"This going out on the buffalo range depends upon the
pay.
But if you will pay good wages and transportation too,
I think, sir, I will go with you to the range of the
buffalo."

"Yes, I will pay good wages, give transportation too,
Provided you will go with me and stay the summer
through;
But if you should grow homesick, come back to
Jacksboro,

I won't pay transportation from the range of the
buffalo."

It's now our outfit was complete—seven able-bodied
men,
With navy six and needle gun—our troubles did begin;
Our way it was a pleasant one, the route we had to go,
Until we crossed Pease River on the range of the
buffalo.

It's now we've crossed Pease River, our troubles have
begun.
The first damned tail I went to rip, Christ! how I cut
my thumb!
While skinning the damned old stinkers our lives wasn't
a show,
For the Indians watched to pick us off while skinning
the buffalo.

He fed us on such sorry truck I wished myself 'most
dead,
It was old jerked beef, croton coffee, and sour bread.
Pease River's as salty as hell fire, the water I could
never go,—
O God! I wished I had never come to the range of the
buffalo.

Our meat it was buffalo hump and iron wedge bread,
And all we had to sleep on was a buffalo robe for a bed;

The fleas and gray-backs worked on us, O boys, it was
  not slow,
I'll tell you there's no worse hell on earth than the
  range of the buffalo.

Our hearts were cased with buffalo hocks, our souls
  were cased with steel,
And the hardships of that summer would nearly make
  us reel.
While skinning the damned old stinkers our lives they
  had no show,
For the Indians waited to pick us off on the hills of
  Mexico.

The season being near over, old Crego he did say
The crowd had been extravagant, was in debt to him
  that day,—
We coaxed him and we begged him and still it was no
  go,—
We left old Crego's bones to bleach on the range of the
  buffalo.

Oh, it's now we've crossed Pease River and homeward
  we are bound,
No more in that hell-fired country shall we ever be
  found.
Go home to our wives and sweethearts, tell others not
  to go,
For God's forsaken the buffalo range and the damned
  old buffalo.

85

THE KINKAIDER'S SONG

You ask what place I like the best,
The sand hills, O the old sand hills;
The place Kinkaiders make their home
And prairie chickens freely roam.

Chorus (for first and second verses):

In all Nebraska's wide domain
'Tis the place we long to see again;
The sand hills are the very best,
She is queen of all the rest.

The corn we raise is our delight,
The melons, too, are out of sight.
Potatoes grown are extra fine
And can't be beat in any clime.

The peaceful cows in pastures dream
And furnish us with golden cream,
So I shall keep my Kinkaid home
And never far away shall roam.

Chorus (third verse):

Then let us all with hearts sincere
Thank him for what has brought us here,
And for the homestead law he made,
This noble Moses P. Kinkaid.

86

DAKOTA LAND

We've reached the land of desert sweet,
Where nothing grows for man to eat.
The wind it blows with feverish heat
Across the plains so hard to beat.

O Dakota land, sweet Dakota land,
As on thy fiery soil I stand
I look across the plains
And wonder why it never rains,
Till Gabriel blows his trumpet sound
And says the rain's just gone around.

We have no wheat, we have no oats,
We have no corn to feed our shoats;
Our chickens are so very poor
They beg for crumbs outside the door.

Our horses are of broncho race;
Starvation stares them in the face.
We do not live, we only stay;
We are too poor to get away.

87

THE DREARY BLACK HILLS

Now friends if you'll listen to a horrible tale
It's getting quite dreary and it's getting quite stale,

I gave up my trade selling Ayers' Patent Pills
To go and hunt gold in the dreary Black Hills.

   Stay away, I say, stay away if you can
   Far from that city they call Cheyenne,
   Where the blue waters roll and Comanche Bill
   Will take off your scalp, boys, in those dreary Black
      Hills.

Now, friends, if you'll listen to a story untold
Don't go to the Black Hills a-digging for gold;
For the railroad speculators their pockets will fill,
While taking you a round trip to the dreary Black Hills.

I went to the Black Hills, no gold could I find.
I thought of the free land I'd left far behind;
Through rain, snow, and hail, boys, froze up to the gills,
They called me the orphan of the dreary Black Hills.

The round house at Cheyenne is filled every night
With loafers and beggars of every kind of sight;
On their backs there's no clothes, boys, in their pockets
    no bills.
And they'll take off your scalp in those dreary Black
    Hills.

88

JOE BOWERS

   My name it is Joe Bowers,
   I've got a brother Ike;

I come from Old Missouri,
It's all the way from Pike.
I'll tell you how I came here,
And how I came to roam,
And leave my good old mammy,
So far away from home.

There was a gal in our town,
Her name was Sally Black;
I asked her for to marry me,
She said it was a whack.
Says she to me, "Joe Bowers,
Before we hitch for life
You ought to have a little home
To keep your little wife."

Says I to her, "Dear Sally!
All for your own dear sake,
I'm off to California
To try to raise a stake."
Says she to me, "Joe Bowers,
You are the man to win,
Here's a kiss to bind the bargain,"
And she threw a dozen in.

When I got to this country
I hadn't nary red.
I had such wolfish feelings,
I almost wished I'as dead.
But when I thought of Sally

It made those feelings git,
And raised the hopes of Bowers—
I wish I had 'em yet.

And so I went to mining,
Put in my biggest licks;
Come down upon the boulders
Like a thousand of bricks.
I labored late and early,
In rain an' sun an' snow,
I was working for my Sally—
'Twas all the same to Joe.

One day I got a letter,
'Twas from my brother Ike;
It came from Old Missouri,
And all the way from Pike.
It was the darndest letter
That ever I did see,
And brought the darndest news
That was ever brought to me.

It said that Sal was false to me—
It made me cuss and swear—
How she'd went and married a butcher,
And the butcher had red hair;
And, whether 'twas gal or boy
The letter never said,
But that Sally had a baby,
And the baby's head was red!

89

IN THE SUMMER OF SIXTY

In the summer of sixty as you very well know
The excitement at Pike's Peak was then all the go;
Many went there with fortunes and spent what they
    had
And came back flat-busted and looking quite sad.

'Twas then I heard farming was a very fine branch,
So I spent most of my money in buying a ranch,
And when I got to it with sorrow and shame
I found a big miner had jumped my fine claim.

So I bought a revolver and swore I'd lay low
The very next fellow that treated me so;
I then went to Denver and cut quite a dash
And took extra pains to show off my cash.

With a fine span of horses, my wife by my side,
I drove through the streets with my hat on one side;
As we were agoin' past the old "Denver Hall"
Sweet music came out that did charm us all.

Says I, "Let's go in and see what's the muss
For I feel right now like having a fuss."
There were tables strung over the hall,
Some was a-whirling a wheel with a ball.

Some playin' cards and some shakin' dice
And lots of half dollars that looked very nice;
I finally strayed to a table at last
Where all the poor suckers did seem to stick fast.

And there stood a man with cards in his hand,
And these were the words which he did command,
"Now, gents, the winning card is the ace,
I guess you will know it if I show you its face."

One corner turned down, it's plain to be seen,
I looked at that fellow and thought he was green,
Yes I looked at that feller and thought he was green,
One corner turned down, 'twas so plain to be seen.

So I bet all my money and lo and behold!
'Twas a tray-spot of clubs and he took all my gold.
Then I went home and crawled into bed
And the divil a word to my wife ever said.

'Twas early next morning I felt for my purse
Biting my lips to keep down a curse;
Yes, 'twas early next morning as the sun did rise
You might have seen with your two blessed eyes,

In an ox wagon, 'twas me and my wife
Goin' down the Platte river for death or for life.

90

THE DYING CALIFORNIAN

Lay up nearer, brother, nearer
  For my limbs are growing cold,
And thy presence seemeth dearer
  When thine arms around me fold.
I am dying, brother, dying,
  Soon you'll miss me in your berth,
And my form will soon be lying
  'Neath the ocean's briny surf.

Harken, brother, closely harken.
  I have something I would say,
Ere the vale my visions darken
  And I go from hence away.
I am going, surely going,
  For my hope in God is strong,
I am willing, brother, knowing
  That he doeth nothing wrong.

Tell my father when you greet him
  That in death I prayed for him,
Prayed that I might one day meet him
  In a world that is free from sin.
Tell my mother God assist her
  Now that she is growing old,
Tell her child would glad have kissed her
  When his lips grew pale and cold.

O my children, heaven bless them,
  They were all my life to me,
Would I could once more caress them
  Ere I sink beneath the sea.
Listen, brother, catch each whisper,
  'Tis my wife I speak of now,
Tell, O tell her how I missed her
  When the fever burned my brow.

Tell her she must kiss my children
  Like the kiss I last impressed.
Hold them as when last I held them
  Folded closely to my breast.
Give them early to their maker,
  Putting all their trust in God,
And he never will forsake them
  For he said so in his word.

Tell my sister when I remember
  Every kindly parting word,
And my heart has been kept tender
  With the thought this memory stirred.
'Twas for them I crossed the ocean—
  What my hopes were I'll not tell;
And I've gained an orphan's portion,
  Yet he doeth all things well.

Tell them I never reach that haven
  Where I sought the "precious dust,"

But I've gained a port called Heaven
   Where the gold will never rust.
Hark, I hear my Saviour speaking,
   'Tis his voice I know so well.
When I am gone, O don't be weeping.
   Brother, here is my last farewell.

MISCELLANEOUS
BALLADS AND SONGS

91

THE PRETTY MOHEA

As I went out walking for pleasure one day,
In sweet recreation to while time away;
As I sat amusing myself on the grass,
O who should I spy but a fair Indian lass.

She sat down beside me, and taking my hand
Said "You are a stranger and in a strange land;
But if you will follow you're welcome to come
And dwell in the cottage that I call my home."

The sun was fast sinking far o'er the blue sea,
When I wandered alone with my pretty Mohea.
Together we wandered, together did rove,
Till we come to the cot in the cocoanut grove.

Then this kind expression she made unto me:
"If you will consent, sir, to stay here with me
And go no more roving upon the salt sea,
I'll teach you the language of the lass of Mohea."

"O no, my dear maiden, that never could be;
For I have a true love in my own country;
And I'll not forsake her for I know she loves me,
And her heart is as true as the pretty Mohea."

'Twas early one morning, a morning in May,
That to this fair maiden these words I did say:

"I'm going to leave you, so farewell my dear;
My ship's sails are spreading and home I must steer."

The last time I saw her she stood on the strand;
And as the boat passed her she waved me her hand,
Saying, "When you have landed with the girl that you
    love,
Think of little Mohea in the cocoanut grove."

And then when I landed on my own native shore,
With friends and relations around me once more,
I gazed all about me—Not one could I see
That was fit to compare with the little Mohea.

And the girl that I trusted proved untrue to me;
So I'll turn my course backward far o'er the deep sea.
I'll turn my course backward; from this land I'll flee;
I'll go spend my days with my pretty Mohea.

92

(A) KATIE'S SECRET

The sunlight is beautiful, mother,
    And bloom the flowers today;
And birds in the branches of hawthorne
    Were carolling ever so gay;
And down by the rock in the meadow
    The rill ripples by with a song,
And, mother, I too have been singing
    The merriest all the day long.

Last night I was weeping, dear mother,
  Last night I was weeping alone,
This world seemed so dark and so dreary
  My heart felt as heavy as stone.
I thought of the lonely and loveless,
  So lonely and loveless was I;
I scarcely know why it was, mother,
  But thought I was wishing to die.

Last night I was weeping, dear mother,
  When Willie came down to the gate,
And whispered, "Come out in the moonlight,
  I've something to say to you, Kate."
And, mother, to him I am dearer
  Than all this wide world beside,
For he told me to sit in the moonlight,
  And called me his darling, his bride.

So now I will gather my roses,
  And twine them in my long braided hair;
And Willie will come in the evening
  And smile when he sees me so fair.
And down by the brookside we'll ramble
  Way down by the great hawthorne tree;
And, mother, I wonder if any
  Were ever so happy as we.

(B) THE HAWTHORNE TREE

Last night I was sleeping, dear mother,
  When Willie came down by the gate;

He whispered, "Come out in the moonlight,
    I've something to say to you, Kate."

We wandered way down in the bushes,
    'Neath the tall old hawthorne tree,
O, mother, I wonder if any were
    Ever so happy as we!

And, mother, to him I am dearer
    Than all in this wide world beside.
He told me so, out in the moonlight,
    He called me his darling, his bride.

And soon they will gather wild flowers,
    To twine in my long braided hair;
Then Willie will come in the evening
    And smile when he sees me so fair.

93

MARY AND WILLIE

As Mary and Willie sat by the sea shore,
    Their last farewell to take,
Said Mary to Willie, "You're now going to sea,
    I fear that my fond heart will break."
"O don't be despairing," young Willie then said,
    And pressed his fair maid to his side;
"My absence don't mourn, for when I return,
    I'll make little Mary my bride."

Three years having passed without any news,
    As Mary stands by her own door,
An old beggar came by with a patch on his eye,
    And did for her pity implore.
"Fair lady," cried he, "your charity bestow,
    And I'll tell your fortune beside;
The lad whom you mourn will never return
    To make little Mary his bride."

"O if it be true you tell unto me,
    My Willie, my hero, still lives,
O if it be true, straightway unto you,
    All the money I have I will give."
"He is living," quoth he, "all in poverty;
    He has been shipwrecked beside;
He'll return no more because he is poor,
    To make little Mary his bride."

"May the heavens above know the joy that I feel,
    And for his misfortune I'll mourn;
He's welcome to me, all in poverty,
    With his blue jacket tattered and torn."
The beggar threw by the patch from his eye,
    Likewise the crutch from his side;
Blue jacket and trousers and cheeks like a rose,
    Young Willie stood by Mary's side.

"Forgive me, fair lady, forgive me," he cried,
    "It was only your love that I tried;
To the church we'll away before close of day,

To make little Mary my bride.
I've money in plenty and riches untold,
    I never was shipwrecked beside;
In coaches we'll roll all covered with gold,
    When I make little Mary my bride."

94

KITTY WELLS

You ask what makes this darkey weep,
    Why he, like others, am not gay,
What makes the tears roll down his cheek
    From early morn till close of day;
My story now you all shall hear,
    For in my memory fond it dwells;
'Twill cause you each to shed a tear
    O'er the grave of my sweet Kitty Wells.

    Where the birds were singing in the morning,
        And the myrtle and the ivy were in bloom,
    While the sun o'er the hill-tops was dawning,
        'Twas there they laid her in her tomb.

I never shall forget the day
    When with sweet Kitty in the dells
I kissed her cheek and named the day
    That I should marry Kitty Wells.
But death came to her cottage door,
    And stole away my joy and pride;
And when I found she was no more,
    I laid my banjo down and cried.

95

PASTORAL ELEGY

What sorrowful sounds do I hear
Move slowly along in the gale?
How solemn the bell on my ear
As softly they pass through the gale!
Sweet Coroden's notes are all o'er,
How lonely he sleeps in the clay!
His cheeks bloom with roses no more
Since death called his spirit away.

Sweet woodbine will rise round his tomb,
And willows there sorrowing wave,
Young hyacinths freshen and bloom
While hawthorns encircle his grave.
Each morn when the sun guiles the east,
The green grass bespangles with dew,
He'll cast his bright beams on the west
To cheer the sad Caroline's view.

O Coroden, hear the sad cries
Of Caroline plaintive and low!
O spirit look down from the skies,
And pity the mourner below!
'Tis Caroline's voice in the grove,
Which Philomel heard on the plain;
Then striving the mourner to soothe,
With sympathy join in her strain.

Ye shepherds so blithesome and young,
Retire from your sports on the green.
Since Coroden's deaf to my song,
The wolves tear the lambs in the plain.
Each swain round the forest will stray,
And sorrowing hung down his head.
His pipe then in sympathy played
Some dirge to young Coroden's shade.

And when the still night has unfurled
Her robes o'er the hamlet around;
Gray twilight retires from the world
And darkness encumbers the ground.
I'll leave my own gloomy abode,
To Coroden's urn will I fly;
Then kneeling will bless the just God
Who dwells in bright mansions on high.

Since Coroden hears me no more
In gloom let the woodlands appear,
Ye oceans, be still of your roar,
Let autumn extend round the year.
I'll hie me through meadows and lawns,
There cull the bright flowers of May;
Then rise on the wings of the morn
And waft my young spirit away.

THE COURTSHIP OF BILLY GRIMES

"Tomorrow, Pa, I'm sweet sixteen, and Billy Grimes
   the drover,
Has popped the question to me, Pa, and wants to be
   my lover;
He's coming here tomorrow, Pa, he's coming bright
   and early,
And I'm to take a walk with him across the fields of
   barley."

"You shall not go, my daughter dear, now there's no
   use in talking;
You shall not go with Billy Grimes across the fields
   a-walking;
To think of such presumption, child, that ugly dirty
   drover,
I don't see where your pride has gone, to think of such
   a lover."

"Old Grimes is dead, you know, Papa, and Billy is
   so lonely,
Old Grimes is dead, you know, Papa, and Billy is the
   only
Surviving heir to all that's left, a good ten thousand
   nearly,
Besides he is the only heir of about three thousand
   yearly."

"I did not hear, my daughter dear, your last remark
    quite clearly,
But Billy is a goodly lad, no doubt he loves you dearly;
Tomorrow morning he may come, he may come bright
    and early,
And you may take a walk with him across the fields of
    barley."

97

FAIR FANNY MOORE

Yonder stands a cottage all deserted and lone,
Its paths are neglected, with grass overgrown,
Go in and you'll see some dark stains on the floor—
Alas! it is the blood of the fair Fanny Moore.

To Fanny so blooming two lovers there came,
One offered young Fanny his wealth and his name;
But neither his money nor pride could secure
A place in the heart of the fair Fanny Moore.

The first was young Randall so bold and so proud,
When to the fair Fanny his haughty head bowed;
But his wealth and his house both failed to allure
The heart from the bosom of fair Fanny Moore.

The next was young Henry of lowest degree,
He won his fond love and enraptured was he;
And then at the altar he quick did secure
The hand and the heart of the fair Fanny Moore.

As she was alone in her cottage one day,
When business had called her fond husband away,
Young Randall the haughty came in at the door,
And clasped in his arms this young fair Fanny Moore.

"Now Fanny, O Fanny, reflect on your fate,
And accept of my offer before 'tis too late;
For one thing tonight I am bound to secure,
'Tis the love or the life of the fair Fanny Moore."

"Spare me, O spare me," the fair Fanny cries,
While the tears swiftly flow from her beautiful eyes;
"O no," says young Randall, "Go home to your rest,"
And he buried his knife in her snowy white breast.

So Fanny all blooming in her bright beauty died,
Young Randall the haughty was taken and tried;
At length he was hung on a tree at the door,
For shedding the blood of the fair Fanny Moore.

Young Henry the shepherd, distracted and wild,
Did wander away from his own native isle;
Till at length claimed by death, he was brought to
the shore
And laid by the side of his fair Fanny Moore.

98

I WISH I WAS SINGLE AGAIN

When I was single, O then, O then,
When I was single, O then,

When I was single, my money did jingle,
I wish I was single again, again,
And I wish I was single again.

I married me a wife, O then, O then,
I married me a wife, O then,
I married me a wife, she's the plague of my life,
And I wished I was single again, again,
And I wished I was single again.

My wife she died, O then, O then,
My wife she died, O then,
My wife she died, and then I cried,
To think I was single again, again,
To think I was single again.

I married another, the devil's grandmother,
I wished I was single again,
For when I was single, my money did jingle,
I wish I was single again, again,
I wish I was single again.

99

I'LL NOT MARRY AT ALL

I'm determined to live an old maid,
I'll take my stool and sit in the shade,
And I'll not marry at all, at all,
    And I'll not marry at all.

O I'll not marry a man who's rich,
For he'd get drunk and fall in a ditch,
And I'll not marry at all, at all,
  And I'll not marry at all.

O I'll not marry a man who's poor,
For he'd go begging from door to door,
And I'll not marry at all, at all,
  And I'll not marry at all.

O I'll not marry a man who chews,
For he'll go slobbering from chin to shoes,
And I'll not marry at all, at all,
  And I'll not marry at all.

O I'll not marry a man who smokes,
For that would not please the old folks,
And I'll not marry at all, at all
  And I'll not marry at all.

Yes, I'm determined to live an old maid,
I'll take my stool and sit in the shade,
And I'll not marry at all, at all,
  And I'll not marry at all.

100

ROSEN THE BOW

I have traveled this wide world all over,
  And now to another I'll go;

For I know that good quarters are waiting
  To welcome Old Rosen the Bow.

The gay round of delight I have travelled,
  Nor will I behind leave a woe;
For when my companions are jovial,
  They drink to Old Rosen the Bow.

This life is now drawing to a closing,
  All will at last be so;
Then we'll take a full bumper at parting,
  To the name of Old Rosen the Bow.

When I am dead and laid out on the counter,
  And the people all anxious to know,
Just raise up the lid of my coffin
  And look at Old Rosen the Bow.

And when through all the streets my friends bear me,
  The ladies are filled with deep woe,
They'll come to the doors and the windows,
  And sigh for Old Rosen the Bow.

Then get me some fine jovial fellows,
  And let them all staggering go;
Then dig a deep hole in the meadow,
  And in it toss Rosen the Bow.

Then get me a couple of dornicks,
  Place one at my head and my toe,

And do not forget to scratch on them,
"Here lies Old Rosen the Bow."

Then let those same jovial fellows,
  Surround my grave in a row,
Whilst they drink from my favorite bottle
The health to old Rosen the Bow.

101

EVALINA

Way down in the meadow where the lily first blows,
Where the wind from the mountain never ruffles the
    rose,
Lives fond Evalina, the sweet little dove,
The pride of the valley, the girl that I love.

    Sweet Evalina, dear Evalina,
    My love for thee will never, never die.

She's fair as the rose, like a lamb she is meek,
And she never was known to put paint on her cheek;
In the most graceful curls hangs her raven black hair,
And she never requires perfumery there.

Evalina and I one fond evening in June,
Took a walk all alone by the light of the moon;
The planets all shone for the heavens were clear,
And I felt round my heart O so mightily queer.

Three years have gone by and I've not got a dollar;
Evalina stills lives in the green grassy hollow;
Although I am fated to marry her never,
I love her, I'm sure, forever and ever.

102

MY BLUE-EYED BOY

There is a tree I love to pass,
And it has leaves as green as grass,
But not as green as love is true;
I love but one and that is you.

Bring to me my blue-eyed boy!
Bring, O bring him back to me!
Bring to me my blue-eyed boy,
What a happy, happy girl I'd be.

Must I go bound and he go free?
Must I love one that don't love me?
Or must I act a childish part
And love the one that broke my heart?

Go bear, go bear, go bear in mind
That a good true friend is hard to find,
And when you find one good and true
Never change the old one for the new.

Adieu, adieu kind friends, adieu,
I can no longer stay with you.
I'll hang my heart in a willow tree,
And give it to the one that first loved me.

103

THE OLD GRAY MULE

Mr. Thomas had an old gray mule,
  And he drove him to a cart,
And he loved that mule and the mule loved him
  With all his mulish heart.
Mr. Thomas knowed when the roosters crowed
  That day was a-gwine to break,
So he slicked that mule with a three-legged stool,
  And he curried him off with a rake.

    And the mule would ea-aw-w-w,
      Ee-aw, ee-aw, ee-aw-w-w,
    And he cuffed that mule and he cuffed that mule,
      And he curried him off with a rake.

He fed him on some old boot tops
  And bits of yellow clay,
Some shavings and some wooden pegs,
  Instead of oats and hay;
And the mule would chaw with his iron jaw,
  On a piece of dirty sock,
And he'd wink his eye if he had some pie,
  And his mouth chuck full of sock.

That mule could kick like a ton of brick;
  Both hind legs were loose,
And he flung them back at a big lipped Jack,
  And he mashed his royal snoot;
That negro thought that he'd been caught
  In an awful big cyclone.
And you bet he wished that he had let
  That old gray mule alone.

One day while wandering in a field
  He found an old hoop skirt;
He at once began to have a feast
  On royal rust and dirt.
That night he had an awful cramp
  That settled in his feet,
And ere morn dawned that mule had gone
  To walk on the golden street.

104

I WILL TELL YOU OF A FELLOW

I will tell you of a fellow,
  Of a fellow I have seen,
Who was neither white nor yellow,
  Nor was altogether green.
      With my life alure a lickem,
      With my life alure a lem.

O he came one night to see me,
　　And he made so long a stay,
That I really thought the blockhead
　　Never meant to go away.
　　　　With my life alure a lickem, etc.

O he told me of devotion,
　　Of devotion pure and deep,
And he talked so awful silly
　　That I nearly fell asleep.
　　　　With my life alure a lickem, etc.

O he told me of a cottage,
　　Of a cottage by the seas,
And then, would you believe it,
　　Why, he tumbled on his knees.
　　　　With my life alure a lickem, etc.

O I knew I couldn't love him,
　　But the very deuce is in it;
For he says if I refuse him,
　　Why, he couldn't live a minute.
　　　　With my life alure a lickem, etc.

And you know the blessed Bible
　　Plainly says we mustn't kill;
So I've thought the matter over,
　　And I kind of think—I will.
　　　　With my life alure a lickem, etc.

105

THE PREACHER'S LEGACY

O, if poor sinners did but know
How much for them I undergo,
They would not treat me with contempt,
Nor curse me when I say "Repent."
Give credit now to what I say,
And mind it till the judgment day,
Of God I'm sent, to you I call,
The invitation is to all.

My loving brethren think it strange
That I should leave my dearest friends;
My sisters wonder where I am,
That I do not return to them.
My parents' house I bid adieu,
And on my journey I pursue,
To distant climes I now repair
To call poor sinners far and near.

Through storms of wind and rain and snow
Both day and night I have to go
To attend the appointments I have made,
Or find some place to lay my head.
Sometimes in open houses sleep
Or in some little place I creep,
I cannot sleep for want of clothes,
Smothered in smoke and almost froze.

I ofttimes with false brethren meet
Whose heart is full of vain deceit.
They seem quite pleasant at the first,
But of all friends they are the worst.
The roaring tempest beat with force,
And ofttimes drives me from my course.
But he who hears the sparrows' care
Protects and drives away my fear.

Sometimes with hunger I grow faint,
But travel on till almost spent,
Without a friend and helper nigh
But he who hears the ravens' cry.
When lo, I hear a glorious voice,
Saying, "Arise, in me rejoice!
Go to the earth's remotest bounds,
I'll be thy friend while foes surround."

And when my work is done below,
I hope to glory I shall go;
I'll take my lofty distant flight
To dwell with saints in endless light,
With all the happy pilgrims there,
And in God's kingdom have a share.
We'll shout and sing, our suffering o'er,
Where Christian friends will part no more.

106

THE SPANISH CABINEER

The Spanish cabineer stood under a tree
And on his gautar played a tone, dear,
The music so sweet I often repeat,
   Remember what I say and be true, dear.

   Say darling, say, when I am far away,
    Sometime you may think of me, dear.
   Bright sunny days, will soon pass away,
    Remember what I say and be true,
    dear.

Off to the war, to the war I must go,
   To fight for my country and you, dear,
And if I should fall, in vain I would call,
   For blessings on you and my country.

When the war is over, to you I'll return,
   Back to my country and you, dear;
But if I am slain you might seek me in vain,
   On the battlefield you will find me.

107

THE TWO DRUMMERS

   Two drummers sat at dinner
   In a grand hotel one day,

While dining they were chatting
　In a jolly sort of way;
And when a pretty waitress
　Brought them a tray of food,
They accosted her
　In a manner rather rude.
At first she did not notice them
　Or make the least reply,
Till one remark was passed
　That brought tears to her eye.
Then, facing her tormentors,
　Cheeks now burning red,
She looked a perfect picture
　As appealingly she said:

　　"My mother was a lady,
　　　As yours, no doubt you'll allow,
　　And you may have a sister
　　　Who needs protection now.
　　I came to this great city
　　　To find a brother dear,
　　You'd not dare insult me, sir,
　　　If Jack were only here."

'Tis true one touch of nature
　Makes the whole world akin,
And every word she uttered
　Seemed to pierce their hearts within.
She left them stunned and silent
　Till just one cry of shame—

"Forgive me, Miss, I meant no harm:
  Pray tell me, what's your name."
She told him and he cried again,
  "I know your brother, too,
We've been friends for many years,
  And he often speaks of you.
He'll be so glad to see you,
  And if you'll only wed,
I'll take you to him as my wife
  For I love you since you said:

  "My mother is a lady,
    As yours, no doubt you'll allow,
  And you may have a sister
    Who needs protection now.
  I came to this great city
    To find a brother dear,
  You'd not dare insult me, sir,
    If Jack were only here."

DIALOGUE, NURSERY,
AND GAME SONGS

108

THE QUAKER'S COURTSHIP

"Madam, I have come a-courting, hi, ho, hum!
I'm for business, not for sporting, hi, ho hum!"

"That you go home is my desire, rol dol dil a day.
Unless you stay and court the fire, rol dol dil a day."

"I've a ring that's worth a shilling, hi ho hum.
Thou mayst wear it if thou'rt willing, hi ho hum!"

"O I don't want your ring or money, rol dol dil a day.
I want a man that'll call me honey, rol dol dil a day."

"I've a kitchen full of servants, hi ho hum!
Thou mayst be a mistress o'er them, hi ho hum."

"Indeed I'll not be scolded for you, rol dol dil a day.
Indeed I think myself above you, rol dol dil a day."

"I've a stable full of horses, hi ho hum,
Thou mayst ride them at my bidding, hi ho hum."

"Indeed I'll not be jockey for you, rol dol dil a day.
I think I'm better off without you, rol dol dil a day."

"Must I give up my religion? O dear me!
Must I join the Presbyterians? O dear me!"

"O you go home and tell your daddy, rol dol dil a day,
That you couldn't get me ready, rol dol dil a day!"

"O you go home and tell your mother, rol dol dil a day,
That you're a fool and lots of bother, rol dol dil a day."

"Must I leave without one token? O dear me!
Must I die with my heart broken? O dear me."

"Cheer up, cheer up, my loving brother, hi ho hum,
If you can't catch me just catch another, hi ho hum!"

109

DUTCHMAN, DUTCHMAN, WON'T YOU MARRY ME?

"Dutchman, Dutchman, won't you marry me?"
    "No, no, no, not I.
How can I marry such a pretty little girl
    When I have no shoes to put on?"

Away to the shoeshop she did vent
    As fast as she could go,
Bought him some shoes of the very best kind.
    "Now, Dutchman, put them on!

"Dutchman, Dutchman, won't you marry me?"
    "No, no, no, not I.
How can I marry such a pretty little girl
    When I have no coat to put on?"

Away to the tailor's shop she did vent
  As fast as she could go,
Bought him a coat of the very best cut.
  "Now Dutchman, draw him on!

"Dutchman, Dutchman, won't you marry me?"
  "No, no, no, not I.
How can I marry such a pretty little girl
  When I have no hat to put on?"

Away to the hatter's shop she did vent
  As fast as she could go,
Bought him a hat of the very best style
  "Now Dutchman, put him on!

"Dutchman, Dutchman, won't you marry me?"
  "No, no, no, not I.
How can I marry such a pretty little girl
  When I have one wife to home?"

110

WHAT WILL YOU GIVE ME IF I GET UP?

  "What will you give me if I get up,
    If I get up, if I get up?
  What will you give me if I get up.
    If I get up today?"

  "A slice of bread and a cup of tea,
    A cup, a cup, a cup of tea,

A slice of bread and a cup of tea,
   If you get up today."

"No, mother, I won't get up,
   I won't, I won't, I won't get up,
No, mother, I won't get up,
   I won't get up today."

"What will you give me if I get up,
   If I get up, if I get up?
What will you give me if I get up,
   If I get up today?"

"A nice young man with rosy cheeks,
   With rosy cheeks, with rosy cheeks,
A nice young man with rosy cheeks,
   If you'll get up today."

"Yes, mother, I will get up,
   I will get up, I will get up,
Yes, mother, I will get up,
   I will get up today."

111

PAPER OF PINS

"I'll give thee a paper of pins
If that's the way that love begins,
If you'll but marry, if you'll but marry, if you'll but
   marry me."

"I'll not accept the paper of pins,
If that's the way that love begins,
And I'll not marry, I'll not marry. I'll not marry you."

"I'll give thee a little lap dog,
That'll go with you when you go abroad,
If you'll but marry, if you'll but marry, if you'll but
    marry me."

"I'll not accept the little lap dog,
To go with me when I go abroad,
And I'll not marry, I'll not marry, I'll not marry you."

"I'll give to thee a coach and four,
With every horse as white as snow,
If you'll but marry, if you'll but marry, if you'll but
    marry me."

"I'll not accept a coach and four,
With every horse as white as snow,
And I'll not marry, I'll not marry, I'll not marry you."

I'll give to thee a coach and six,
With every horse as black as pitch,
If you'll but marry, if you'll but marry, if you'll but
    marry me."

"I'll not accept the coach and six,
With every horse as black as pitch,
And I'll not marry, I'll not marry, I'll not marry you."

"I'll give to thee the key of my heart,
That we may lock and never part,
If you'll but marry, if you'll but marry, if you'll but
    marry me."

"I'll not accept the key of thy heart,
That we may lock and never part,
And I'll not marry, I'll not marry, I'll not marry you."

"I'll give to thee a chest of gold,
And all the money you can control,
If you'll but marry, if you'll but marry, if you'll but
    marry me."

"I will accept a chest of gold,
And all the money I can control,
And I will marry, I will marry, I will marry you."

"Ha, ha! Ha, ha! money is all
Woman's love is nothing at all,
And I'll not marry, I'll not marry, I'll not marry you."

112

(A) THE MILKMAID

"Where are you going, my pretty maid,
    My pretty maid, my pretty maid,
Where are you going, my pretty maid?"
"I'm going a-milking, sir, I say,

Sir, I say, sir, I say,
I'm going a-milking, sir, I say."

"May I go with you, my pretty maid,
   My pretty maid, my pretty maid,
May I go with you, my pretty maid?"
"You may if you wish to, sir, I say,
   Sir, I say, sir, I say,
You may if you wish to, sir, I say."

"What is your father, my pretty maid,
   My pretty maid, my pretty maid,
What is your father, my pretty maid?"
"My father's a farmer, sir, I say,
   Sir, I say, sir, I say,
My father's a farmer, sir, I say."

"What is your fortune, my pretty maid,
   My pretty maid, my pretty maid,
What is your fortune, my pretty maid?"
"My face is my fortune, sir, I say,
   Sir, I say, sir, I say,
My face is my fortune, sir, I say."

"Then I won't have you, my pretty maid,
   My pretty maid, my pretty maid,
Then I won't have you, my pretty maid."
"Nobody asked you, sir, I say,
   Sir, I say, sir, I say,
Nobody asked you, sir, I say."

(B) THE PRETTY MILKMAID

"O where are you going to, my pretty maid,
O where are you going to, my pretty maid?"
"I'm going a-milking, sir," she said, "sir," she said,
"I'm going a-milking, sir," she said.

"O may I go with you, my pretty maid,
O may I go with you, my pretty maid?"
"O yes, if you like, kind sir," she said, "sir," she said,
"O yes, if you like, kind sir," she said.

"O what is your father, my pretty maid,
O what is your father, my pretty maid?"
"My father's a farmer, sir," she said, "sir," she said,
"My father's a farmer, sir," she said.

"O what is your fortune, my pretty maid,
O what is your fortune, my pretty maid?"
"My face is my fortune, sir," she said, "sir," she said,
"My face is my fortune, sir," she said.

"Then I cannot marry you, my pretty maid,
I cannot marry you, my pretty maid,"
"O nobody axed you, sir," she said, "sir," she said,
"O nobody axed you, sir," she said.

113

BILLY BOY

"O where have you been Billy Boy, Billy Boy,
  O where have you been, charming Billy?"
"I have been for a wife, she's the treasure of my life,
  She's a young thing but can't leave her mammie."

"Can she make a cherry pie, Billy Boy, Billy Boy,
  Can she make a cherry pie, charming Billy?"
"She can make a cherry pie quick as cat can wink her
    eye,
  She's a young thing but can't leave her mammie."

"Can she make a feather bed, Billy Boy, Billy Boy,
  Can she make a feather bed, charming Billy?"
"She can make it very neat from the head unto the
    feet,
  She's a young thing but can't leave her mammie."

"Can she make a loaf of bread, Billy Boy, Billy Boy
  Can she make a loaf of bread, charming Billy?"
"She can make a loaf of bread with a night cap on
    her head,
  She's a young thing but can't leave her mammie."

"Can she milk a mulie cow, Billy Boy, Billy Boy,
  Can she milk a mulie cow, charming Billy?"

"She can milk a mulie cow if her mammie shows her
   how.
She's a young thing but can't leave her mammie."

114

POOR ROBIN

Poor Robin was dead and lay in his grave,
   Lay in his grave, lay in his grave,
Poor Robin was dead and lay in his grave,
   O O O O.

They planted an apple tree over his head,
   Over his head, over his head,
They planted an apple tree over his head,
   O O O O.

When the apples were ripe and ready to fall,
   Ready to fall, ready to fall,
When the apples were ripe and ready to fall,
   O O O O.

An old woman came and gathered them up,
   Gathered them up, gathered them up,
An old woman came and gathered them up,
   O O O O.

Poor Robin jumped up and gave her a thump,
   Gave her a thump, gave her a thump.

Poor Robin jumped up and gave her a thump.
  O O O O.

It made the old woman go flippety flop,
  Flippety flop, flippety flop,
It made the old woman go flippety flop,
  O O O O.

And as she ran off her apron string broke,
  Her apron string broke, her apron string broke,
And as she ran off her apron string broke.
  O O O O.

If you want any more just sing it yourself,
  Sing it yourself, sing it yourself;
If you want any more just sing it yourself,
  O O O O.

115

BABES IN THE WOODS

My dear you must know that a long time ago
There was two little children whose names I don't
    know,
Who were taken away on a bright autumn day,
And lost in the woods I have heard people say.

Now when it was night very sad were their plight,
The stars did not shine and the moon hid her light,

Then they sobbed and they sighed and sadly they cried,
And the poor little things at last lay down and died.

Two robins so red when they saw them lie dead
Brought beech and oak leaves and over them spread;
And all day long the branches among
They sang to them softly and this was their song:

> Poor little babes in the woods,
> Poor little babes in the woods,
> O who will come and find,
> Poor little babes in the woods!

116

IN GOOD OLD COLONY TIMES

In good old colony times, where we lived under the
King,
  Three roguish chaps fell into mishaps
Because they could not sing.
  Three roguish chaps fell into mishaps
Because they could not sing.

The first he was a miller, and the second he was a weaver,
  And the third he was a little tailor,
Three roguish chaps together,
  And the third he was a little tailor,
Three roguish chaps together.

The miller he stole corn, and the weaver he stole yarn,
  And the little tailor stole broadcloth
For to keep these three rogues warm.
  And the little tailor stole broadcloth
For to keep these three rogues warm.

Now the miller got drowned in his dam, and the weaver
    got hung in his yarn,
  And the devil clapt his claws on the little tailor
With the broadcloth under his arm,
  And the devil clapt his claws on the little tailor,
With the broadcloth under his arm.

117
LET'S GO TO THE WOODS

"Let's go to the woods," says Richard to Robin,
"Let's go to the woods," says Robin to Bobin,
"Let's go to the woods," says Johnny alone,
"Let's go to the woods," says every one.

"What to do there?" says Richard to Robin,
"What to do there?" says Robin to Bobin,
"What to do there?" says Johnny alone,
"What to do there?" says everyone.

"Shoot at my wren," says Richard to Robin,
"Shoot at my wren," says Robin to Bobin,
"Shoot at my wren," says Johnny alone,
"Shoot at my wren," says every one.

"What if she's dead?" says Richard to Robin,
"What if she's dead?" says Robin to Bobin,
"What if she's dead?" says Johnny alone,
"What if she's dead?" says every one.

"How would you get her home?" says Richard to
    Robin,
"How would you get her home?" says Robin to Bobin,
"How would you get her home?" says Johnny alone,
"How would you get her home?" says every one.

"A cart and six horses," says Richard to Robin,
"A cart and six horses," says Robin to Bobin,
"A cart and six horses," says Johnny alone,
"A cart and six horses," says every one.

118

I BOUGHT ME A WIFE

I bought me a wife the tenth of June,
    Nickety nackety, now, now, now,
I brought her home by the light of the moon.
    High, willy, wally, and Jenny bang,
    Doodle, sandy go restego, now, now, now.

I bought two cows, they both were good,
I told her to milk whichever she would.

For want of a churn she used the old man's boot,
For want of a dasher she used his foot.

She made some cheese and hung it on a pin.
The grease ran out and the dirt sucked in.

The old book lies on the shelf.
If you want any more you can sing it yourself.

119

WE'LL ALL GO DOWN TO ROWSER'S

We'll all go down to Rowser's,
We'll all go down to Rowser's,
We'll all go down to Rowser's,
    For there they keep the beer,
    For there they keep the beer,
    For there they keep the beer,
We'll all go down to Rowser's
    For there they keep the beer.

My father and mother were Irish,
My father and mother were Irish,
My father and mother were Irish,
    And I was Irish too,
    And I was Irish too,
    And I was Irish too.
My father and mother were Irish
    And I was Irish too.

They kept the pig in the parlor,
They kept the pig in the parlor,
They kept the pig in the parlor,

For that was Irish too,
For that was Irish too,
For that was Irish too.
They kept the pig in the parlor,
For that was Irish too.

120

SWEET FIELDS OF VIOLO

How happy I was on my father's farm,
  Sweet fields of Violo,
Tending to my father's horses
That I fed in the barns of Violo.
  And a gee ho here and a gee ho there,
  Here a gee and there a gee, and
O pretty maids, won't you come and go with me
  To the sweet fields of Violo!

How happy I was on my father's farm,
  Sweet fields of Violo,
Tending to my father's cows
That I milked in the yards of Violo.
  And a suke, suke here, and a suke, suke there,
  Here a suke and there a suke, and
  A gee ho here and a gee ho there,
  Here a gee and there a gee, and
O pretty maids, won't you come and go with me
  To the sweet fields of Violo!

How happy I was on my father's farm,
  Sweet fields of Violo,

Tending to my father's pigs
That I fattened in the pens of Violo.
   And a boo hoo here and a boo hoo there,
   Here a boo and there a boo, and
   A suke suke here and a suke suke there,
   Here a suke and there a suke, and
   A gee ho here and a gee ho there,
   Here a gee and there a gee, and
O pretty maids, won't you come and go with me
   To the sweet fields of Violo!

How happy I was on my father's farm,
   Sweet fields of Violo,
Tending to my father's sheep
That ran in the vales of Violo.
   And a bleat bleat here, and a bleat bleat there,
   Here a bleat and there a bleat, and
   A boo hoo here and a boo hoo there,
   Here a boo and there a boo, and
   A suke suke here and a suke suke there,
   Here a suke and there a suke, and
   A gee ho here and a gee ho there,
   Here a gee and there a gee, and
O pretty maids, won't you come and go with me
   To the sweet fields of Violo!

How happy I was on my father's farm,
   Sweet fields of Violo,
Tending to my father's geese
That swam in the ponds of Violo.
   With a shoo shoo here and a shoo shoo there,

Here a shoo and there a shoo, and
A bleat bleat here and a bleat bleat there,
Here a bleat and there a bleat, and
A boo hoo here and a boo hoo there,
Here a boo and there a boo, and
A suke suke here and a suke suke there,
Here a suke and there a suke, and
A gee ho here and a gee ho there,
Here a gee and there a gee, and
O pretty maids, won't you come and go with me
To the sweet fields of Violo!

How happy I was on my father's farm,
Sweet fields of Violo.
Tending to my father's chickens
That laid in the nests of Violo.
A cackle cackle here and a cackle cackle there,
Here a cackle, there a cackle, and
A shoo shoo here and a shoo shoo there,
Here a shoo and there a shoo, and
A bleat bleat here and a bleat bleat there,
Here a bleat and there a bleat, and
A boo hoo here and a boo hoo there,
Here a boo and there a boo, and
A suke suke here and a suke suke there,
Here a suke and there a suke, and
A gee ho here and a gee ho there,
Here a gee and there a gee, and
O pretty maids, won't you come and go with me
To the sweet fields of Violo!

NOTES

1. (A) JOHNNY RANDALL. Compare *Lord Randal*, Child, *English and Scottish Popular Ballads*, No. 12. Text recovered by Professor H. C. House of the University of Maryland from a railroad camp at Geary, Colorado, in 1901. See *Modern Language Notes*, vol. 17, p. 14, 1902.

(B) JIMMY RANDOLPH. Sung by Mrs. Dora Shelton, Allenstand, North Carolina, in 1916. See Campbell and Sharp, *English Folk Songs from the Southern Appalachians*, p. 22.

2. (A) LORD LOVEL. Text obtained from S. J. Mason of Lincoln, Nebraska, in 1906, who "learned it at Aledo, Illinois, about 1863." Child, No. 75.

(B) LORD LOVER. Text obtained from Mrs. Jeanetta Gear of Junction, Wyoming, in 1914.

3. (A) BARBERY ALLEN. Text as sung and transcribed by Miss Stella Cotton of Miller County, Missouri. See H. M. Belden, "Old Country Songs in Missouri," *Journal of American Folk-Lore*, vol. 19, p. 287. 1906. Child, No. 84.

(B) BARBARA ALLEN. Text from North Carolina. Secured by Miss Mary Crawford of the State Normal School at Kearney, Nebraska, in 1913.

4. (A) THE TWO SISTERS. Sung by Mrs. Jane Gentry of Hot Springs, North Carolina, in 1916. See Campbell and Sharp, *English Folk Songs from the Southern Appalachians* (1917), p. 16. Child, No. 10. This ballad is known to Miss Marjorie Burcham of Lincoln, Nebraska, as a eucalele song.

(B) THE OLD MAN IN THE NORTH COUNTRY. Text brought to Clinton County, Missouri, from Kentucky. See H. M. Belden, "Old Country Ballads in Missouri," *Journal of American Folk-Lore*, vol. 19, p. 233. 1906.

5. (A) THE JEWISH LADY. Compare *Sir Hugh*, or *The Jew's Daughter* Child, No. 155. Secured by Mrs. Pearl H. Bartholomew from Mrs. Flo Keller, both of Warren, Indiana. See A. H. Tolman, "Some Songs Traditional in the United States," *Journal of American Folk-Lore*, vol. 29, p. 165. 1916.

(B) THE JEW LADY. Text secured at the University of Virginia by C. Alphonso Smith. It was learned at Montgomery, Alabama. See "Ballads Surviving in the United States," *The Musical Quarterly*, January, 1916, p. 16. Title supplied.

6. (A) THE WIFE WRAPT IN WETHER'S SKIN. Text secured by H. M. Belden in 1916 from Mrs. Eva Warner Case of Kansas City, "as known to her in her childhood in Harrison County, Missouri, about 1890." Child, No. 277.

(B) DANDOO. Text from Mrs. Mary A. Sexson of Hastings, Nebraska, in 1917, as sung by her husband, J. J. Sexson.

7. (A) CHILDREN'S SONG. Compare *The Wife of Usher's Well,* Child, No. 79. Text secured by Walter Morris Hart from Mrs. Agnes McDougall Henry, who had it from western North Carolina. See G. L. Kittredge, "Ballads and Songs," *Journal of American Folk-Lore,* vol. 30, p. 306. 1917.

(B) THREE LITTLE BABES. Secured by L. A. Quivey when a student at the University of Nebraska, as known to his family in Burt County, Nebraska, in 1914.

8. THE CRUEL BROTHER. Text from Boston Massachusetts. See Phillips Barry, "The Ballad of the Cruel Brother," *Journal of American Folk-Lore,* vol. 28, p. 300. 1915. Child, No. 11.

9. EDWARD. Sung by Mrs. Jane Gentry at Hot Springs, North Carolina, in 1916. Campbell and Sharp, *English Folk Songs from the Southern Appalachians,* p. 26.

10. THE LOWLANDS LOW. Compare *The Sweet Trinity,* Child, No. 286. Sung by James R. Barron of Lincoln, Nebraska, in 1919. Mr. Barron is from the Shetland Islands. Secured by L. C. Wimberly.

11. THREE SAILOR BOYS. Compare *The Mermaid,* Child, No. 289. From Mrs. Jeanetta Gear, Junction, Wyoming, 1914.

12. LORD THOMAS. Compare Lord Thomas and Fair Annet, Child, No. 73. Secured by Miss Florence Grimm of Lincoln, Nebraska, in 1913, from her grandfather, who brought it from Maryland.

13. THE HANGMAN'S SONG. Compare *The Maid Freed from the Gallows,* Child, No. 95. Text from *Lonesome Tunes* by Loraine Wyman and Howard Brockway (1916), p. 44. From Knott County, Kentucky.

14. LORD BAYHAM. Compare *Young Beichan,* Child, No. 53. Text from a manuscript book of songs, made from oral transcription in Indiana before the Civil War, in the possession of Edna Fulton Waterman of Lincoln, Nebraska. The American variants of this ballad have many titles, "Young Bakeman," "Lord Batesman," "Lord Bateman," "Lord Bacon," "Lord Benham," "The Turkish Lady," etc. This ballad was a favorite with Dickens. Much of its currency is due to the fact that it was utilized with effect in the once popular play of *Rosedale.* See G. L. Kittredge in *Harvard Library Notes,* January, 1921, p. 62.

15. LITTLE MATTHY GROVES. Compare *Little Musgrave and Lady Barnard,* Child, No. 81. Sung by Mrs. Jane Gentry of Hot Springs, North Carolina, in 1916. Campbell and Sharp, *English Folk Songs from the Southern Appalachians,* p. 79. This ballad has been found in Nova Scotia by W. Roy Mackenzie, by H. G. Shearin in the Cumberland Mountains, and by C. Alphonso Smith ("Little Mosie Grove and Lord Burnett's Wife," etc.) in Virginia.

16. SWEET WILLIAM. Compare *Fair Margaret and Sweet William*, Child, No. 74. Text from Josephine McGill's *Folk Songs of the Kentucky Mountains* (1917), p. 69.

17. THE HOUSE CARPENTER. Compare *James Harris*, or *The Dœmon Lover*, Child, No. 243. Text obtained in 1908 from S. J. Mason of Lincoln, Nebraska, who learned it as a boy at Aledo, Illinois.

18. TWO LITTLE BOYS. Compare *The Two Brothers*, Child, No. 49. Secured in 1909 by her daughter from Mrs. Eliza Shelman of Hansen's Ferry, Washington, who learned it in Nodaway County, Missouri.

19. THE CHERRY TREE CAROL. Text from Josephine McGill's *Folk Songs of the Kentucky Mountains*, p. 59. Child, No. 54.

20. THE FALSE KNIGHT. Compare Child, No. 3. Secured by H. M. Belden in 1916 from Miss J. D. Johns of St. Charles, Missouri. She learned it from her uncle, Mr. Douglas Voss Martin, who learned it when a boy in Virginia from his grandmother, a Scotchwoman. See Kittredge, "Ballads and Songs," *Journal of American Folk-Lore*, vol. 30, p. 286. 1917.

21. (A) THE DROWSY SLEEPER. Text from a manuscript book of songs from oral transcription, the property of Edna Fulton Waterman of Lincoln, Nebraska. For this piece, see H. M. Belden, *Archiv für das Studium der neueren Sprachen*, vol. 119, pp. 430-431.

(B) WILLIE AND MARY. Text known to Mrs. I. E. Diehl of Robinson, Utah, 1914.

22. (A) THE BAMBOO BRIARS. Text from H. M. Belden, who had it from Miss Frances Barbour of Washington University, who had it from the singing of Minnie Doyle of Arlington, Phelps County, Missouri, in 1917. For the history of this song, and variant texts, see H. M. Belden, "Boccaccio, Hans Sachs, and *The Bramble Briar*," *Publications of the Modern Language Association* of America, vol. 33, p. 327. 1918.

(B) THE APPRENTICE BOY. Text of H. G. Shearin. See "British Ballads in the Cumberland Mountains," *The Sewanee Review*, vol. 19, p. 321. July, 1911.

23. (A) THE BOSTON BURGLAR. Text obtained by L. C. Wimberly from Mrs. E. N. Hardin, of Missouri Valley, Iowa, in 1916. Compare *The Sheffield Apprentice*, Campbell and Sharp, *English Folk Songs from the Southern Appalachians*, p. 278. A text of this song from Michigan adapts it, with a minimum of changes, to fit a local crime and criminal in Michigan.

(B) CHARLESTON. Text obtained from Harry Gear, Junction, Wyoming, 1914.

24. (A) THE BUTCHER'S BOY. Text obtained by Lillian Gear Boswell at Hartville, Wyoming, 1914. Related to *The Brisk Young*

Lover, Broadwood, *Traditional Songs and Carols* (1908), p. 92. See also, Campbell and Sharp, p. 286.

(B) THERE IS A TAVERN IN THE TOWN. From a manuscript book of songs in the possession of L. C. Wimberly. 1916. This well-known college song is a variant of, or is somehow related to, *The Brisk Young Lover* and *The Butcher's Boy.*

25. THE DEATH OF A ROMISH LADY. From a manuscript book of orally transcribed pieces, the property of Edna Fulton Waterman of Lincoln, Nebraska. This piece has been found also in Missouri and in the Cumberland Mountains. It is the "It was a lady's daughter of Paris properly" mentioned in Fletcher's *Knight of the Burning Pestle* (1613), V. iii. A text from the time of Charles II appears in *The Roxburgh Ballads*, vol. I, p. 43.

26. JOHNNY AND BETSY. Text of Mrs. Mary F. Lindsay of Hebron, Nebraska. 1915. Compare Firth, *An American Garland* (1915), p. 69. A text from California is printed in *The Journal of American Folk-Lore*, vol. 19, p. 130, but the account there given of the origin of the song is doubtful.

27. THE SOLDIER. Text from Mrs. B. B. Wimberly, 1916, who learned it in Louisiana. Compare Campbell and Sharp, *The Lady and the Dragoon*, p. 161. The same story is told in the last part of *The Masterpiece of Love Songs* in John Ashton's *A Century of Ballads* (1887), p. 164. Professor Tolman has pointed out that the story somewhat resembles that of *Erlinton*, Child, No. 8.

28. THE FARMER'S BOY. Text from Miss Frances Francis of Cheyenne, Wyoming, who had it from her father, who described it as "brought from Newcastle, England, as early as 1870." Known also in Missouri.

29. THE RICH YOUNG FARMER. From Edna Fulton Waterman's manuscript book of ballads, in which it is transcribed as "Written by Marcelia Polk at E. Spencer's school, the 23rd of February, 1857." Compare H. G. Shearin's *William Hall* from the Cumberland mountains. For ballads current in America on the theme of the returned lover, see H. M. Belden, *Archiv fur das Studium der neueren Sprachen und Literaturen*, vol. 120, p. 62.

30. THE LOVER'S RETURN. From Mrs. Waterman's manuscript book of songs. Reproduced *literatim*. A version of the widely current *The Banks of Claudy*. See *Journal of American Folk-Lore* vol. 26, p. 362. 1913.

31. THE PRENTICE BOY. From Mrs. Waterman's manuscript book of ballads from Indiana, in which it bears the date 1844. Reproduced *literatim*. Compare *The Lady and the Prentice*, Baring-Gould, *Songs of the West* (1913), p. 219. For American variants see *The Journal of American Folk-Lore*, vol. 26, p. 363. 1913.

32. THE CONSTANT FARMER'S SON. Text from L. C. Wimberly of

Lincoln, Nebraska, in 1916. H. M. Belden prints a text in *The Sewanee Review*, vol. 19, p. 222, and in the *Publications of the Modern Language Association of America*, vol. 33, p. 367, 1918; and W. R. Mackenzie in *The Quest of the Ballad*.

33. MOLLIE BOND. Miss Loraine Wyman's text, printed by G. L. Kittredge in the *Journal of American Folk-Lore*, vol. 30, p. 359. Compare "Polly Bam" in *The Shooting of His Dear*, Campbell and Sharp, p. 159. Known also as "Polly Vann," "Molly Baun," "Polly Vaughn," etc. According to Professor Kittredge, this piece is at least as old as the eighteenth century. Possibly it is much older. The transformation of the girl into a swan and her appearance in court in some of the British versions (instead of as a ghost in certain American versions) point to early origin. See *At the Setting of the Sun* in Baring-Gould's *Songs of the West*, p. 129.

34. MY FATHER'S GRAY MARE. Text obtained from Vivian Cleaver Cleveland of Lincoln, Nebraska, in 1917. Compare Baring-Gould, *Songs of the West*, p. 105 (1913), Kidson, *Traditional Tunes*, etc.

35. MARY O' THE WILD MOOR. Text transcribed by Mrs. Nellie B. Pickup of Lincoln, Nebraska, in 1914, from the singing of her mother, who learned it in her childhood in New York. It is included in Helen K. Johnson's *Our Familiar Songs* (1904), p. 303. See also Kidson's *Traditional Tunes* (1891), p. 77.

36. FATHER GRUMBLE. Text obtained from Miss Jeanne Allen of Seneca, Kansas, in 1914. Known also as "Old Grumble," "The Drummer and his Wife" (Campbell and Sharp, p. 308), etc. The song is no recent one. See Kittredge's annotation, *Journal of American Folk-Lore*, vol. 26, p. 366, 1913.

37. GUY FAWKES. Text known to A. J. Leach of Oakdale, Antelope County, Nebraska, 1914, who learned it as a boy in Michigan. A much better known Guy Fawkes song begins, "O don't you remember the fifth of November."

38. WILLIAM REILLY'S COURTSHIP. From Edna Fulton Waterman's manuscript ballad book.

39. JACK RILEY. Obtained by Frances Botkin and Zora Schaupp from Mrs. Adna Dobson of Lincoln, Nebraska, who learned it in England.

40. THE BATTLE OF POINT PLEASANT. Song included with other traditional songs in Kate Aplington's *Pilgrims of the Plains* (1913), p. 209. She says of its singers: "There are many among them who cannot read, and for those who can there are no newspapers or books. The time would hang heavy on their hands if one did not take it upon himself to help entertain the others. They are capital story tellers and they are all of them singers, and they give themselves up

to the spell of the music with a whole-hearted enthusiasm that gives
to their rudest ballads something of charm and power."

41. JAMES BIRD. This song of a hero of the war of 1812 was known
to S. B. Pound of Lincoln, Nebraska, who brought it from Ontario
County, New York. H. M. Belden has a copy from Clinton County,
Missouri, written down in 1915. It was composed in 1814 by
Charles Miner, of Wilkesbarre, Pennsylvania.

42. (A) O JOHNNY DEAR, WHY DID YOU GO? Secured by Marie
Gladys Hayden of Hobson, Montana, in 1914 from E. B. Lyon, who
reported the song as he heard it sung in a log schoolhouse in Illinois
in the year 1857. This song dates from the eighteenth century and
grew out of a local event. See "Elegy of a Young Man Bitten by a
Rattlesnake" in E. E. Hale's *New England History in Ballads* (1904),
p. 86. See also *The Journal of American Folk-Lore*, vol. 13, pp.
105-112; vol. 18, pp. 295-302; vol. 22, pp. 366-67; vol. 28, p. 169.
The original text is in existence, and the variants of this song, from
different regions well exhibit what has happened to it in more than
a century of oral, transmission and migration.

(B) [WOODVILLE MOUND.] Text secured for H. M. Belden by
Miss G. M. Hamilton from Marie Walt, one of her pupils in the West
Plains, Missouri, High School in 1909, who knew it as sung to her in
her childhood by her mother. Title supplied.

(C) IN SPRINGFIELD MOUNTAIN. Text sent to H. M. Belden
by Miss G. M. Hamilton, who secured it from one of her students at
the Kirksville Normal School, Missouri, in 1911.

(D) SPRINGFIELD MOUNTAIN. Text secured by Frances
Botkin and Zora Schaupp from Mrs. Adna Dobson of Lincoln,
Nebraska, in 1920.

43. (A) THE JEALOUS LOVER. From a manuscript book of ballads
in the possession of L. C. Wimberly, 1916. This is one of the most
widespread of American ballads. It is current under many names, as
"Lorella," "Floella," "Florilla," "Flora Ella," "Poor Lurella,"
"Poor Lora," "Poor Lorla," "Nell," etc. Professor J. H. Cox has
pointed out that the West Virginia "Pearl Bryan" is an adaptation
of this song, with a minimum of verbal changes, to fit the murder
of a girl of that name which occurred near Fort Thomas, Kentucky,
in 1896. The song had an ephemeral popularity after the execution
of the murderers.

(B) THE WEEPING WILLOW. Obtained by Lillian Gear Boswell from the singing of Albert Clay of Junction, Wyoming, in 1914.

44. YOUNG CHARLOTTE. Text obtained by Marie Gladys Hayden
of Hobson, Montana, from the singing of a girl from Plainville,
Kansas, in 1914. For the history of this song, which was composed
in Bensontown, Vermont, before 1835 and grew out of a local event,
see Phillips Barry, *Journal of American Folk-Lore*, vol. 25, p. 156,

1912. Mr. Barry believes that it was carried over the country as its author went to Ohio and later to Illinois, on his way to join the Mormons in Utah. It is widely current.

45. (A) THE OLD SHAWNEE. Text from a manuscript book in the possession of L. C. Wimberly, 1916.

(B) ON THE BANKS OF THE OLD PEDEE. The same song, as obtained from Lillian Gear Boswell at Junction, Wyoming, 1915.

46. THE YOUNG MAN WHO WOULDN'T HOE CORN. Text secured from Bessie Aten when a student at the University of Nebraska in 1914. The song is sometimes known as "Harm Link." See Campbell and Sharp, *English Folk Songs of the Southern Appalachians,* p. 314; *Journal of American Folk Lore,* vol. 29, p. 181. A. H. Tolman's text of the same piece goes under the name of *The Lazy Man.*

47. WICKED POLLY. Text from E. F. Piper, who had it from Mrs. Lydia Hinshaw of Richland, Iowa. The second text is one of four printed by P. Barry, *Modern Language Notes,* vol. 28, p. 1. A. H. Tolman has a version in *The Journal of American Folk-Lore,* vol. 29, p. 192, 1916.

48. JOHNNY SANDS. The first text is from a manuscript book of songs obtained by Grace Munson of Chicago from Mrs. Woodruff of Weston Road, Wellesley, in 1916. The second text is from Harry Gear, of Junction, Wyoming, 1914. For this song see A. H. Tolman, "Some Songs Traditional in the United States," *Journal of American Folk-Lore,* vol. 29, p. 178, with Kittredge's annotations. It belongs to the forties of the nineteenth century. It achieved enormous vogue in this country, says Professor Kittredge, by forming part of the repertory of the Hutchinson Family, the Continental Vocalists, and other singing "troupes."

49. FULLER AND WARREN. Obtained from Jane Andrews of Cambridge, Nebraska, in 1915. Miss Andrews made this comment: "This song was sung in 1874 by some young men in western Nebraska who had come from the vicinity in which this really happened."

50. POOR GOINS. Obtained by G. L. Kittredge from Loraine Wyman "as sung by Rob Morgan, Hindman, Kentucky, in 1916." See "Songs and Ballads," *Journal of American Folk-Lore,* vol. 30, p. 361, 1917.

51. POOR OMIE. From the singing of Mr. Hilliard Smith at Hindman, Kentucky, 1909. See Campbell and Sharp, *English Folk Songs from the Southern Appalachians,* p. 228. Professor H. M. Belden has a copy of *Omie Wise (Poor Omie)* from Earl Cruikshank, with the following account: "This song was handed down to my mother through her grandfather who came from Virginia. My mother says that he was acquainted with Omie Wise and had danced with her and went in the same circle with her. He described her as being a small light-complexioned girl. One time when he sang this song at a

literary meeting or singing school in Indiana, there was a stranger
at the meeting who got up and left the meeting and skipped the
country. Many people thought perhaps this man might have been
the Lewis who murders Omie in the song."

52. SILVER DAGGER. The first text was secured by Lillian Gear
Boswell from the singing of Myrtle Smith Badger of Junction, Wyoming, in 1914. The second text was learned in Mackinaw, Illinois,
by Mrs. Mary F. Lindsay of Hebron, Nebraska.

53. THE AGED INDIAN. Text from Mrs. E. N. Hardin of Missouri
Valley, Iowa, 1916. A fragment of the same song from Red Cloud,
Nebraska (1915) bears the title "Uncle Tohido." H. M. Belden's
Missouri text is named "Uncle Tahia."

54. CALOMEL. Obtained by E. F. Piper of Iowa City from a
manuscript book of ballads in the possession of Mrs. Lydia Hinshaw
of Richland, Iowa, as it was sung by the latter's mother when she
came from Ohio to Iowa in 1840. The song is still alive in fragment,
or shortened versions. A copy in a manuscript book from Indiana,
the property of Edna Fulton Waterman, has for the date of its transcription 1844. Possibly of British importation.

55. THE CREOLE GIRL. Obtained by E. F. Piper from Ival
McPeak, who learned it from the singing of his father in Iowa.

56. THE BLUE AND THE GRAY. Text from L. C. Wimberly's
manuscript book, 1916. One of the most widely current of the
songs remaining from the Cuban War.

57. THE GAMBLER. Secured for H. M. Belden by Miss Frances
Barbour, Washington University, from the singing of Minnie Doge
at Arlington, Phelps County, Missouri, in 1917.

58. IN THE BAGGAGE COACH AHEAD. Text obtained from Blanche
Pope of Red Cloud, Nebraska, in 1914. According to *The Literary
Digest*, November 13, 1915, *In the Baggage Coach Ahead* was one of
the songs sung in vaudeville circuits to the accompaniment of colored
pictures thrown on the screen—"pictures as honest and whole-
hearted in their coloring as they were heart-rending in subject."

59. CASEY JONES. Phillips Barry writes of this song that Casey
Jones was John Luther Jones, engineer of the Chicago and New
Orleans Limited, who was killed in a wreck March 18, 1900. The
song was composed by a negro, Wallace Saunders. See *The Railroad
Man's Magazine*, November, 1910. The version printed here is
from the issue of May 1918 of the same periodical. The vaudeville
version was published in 1909 as the composition of T. L. Seibert and
E. Newton. It was one of the "hits" of the day. This accounts
for the currency of the ballad.

60. THE LADY ELGIN. Text as sung on a ranch at Junction,
Wyoming. Obtained by Lillian Gear Boswell in 1914. This song
is by Henry C. Work and commemorates a wreck on Lake Michigan

in 1860. The singers had no knowledge whatever of its authorship
and origin.

61. THE JAMESTOWN FLOOD. Text known to May B. Wimberly of
Lincoln, 1917. The subject is plainly the Johnstown flood of 1890,
but the title as given by Mrs. Wimberly is retained.

62. THE MILWAUKEE FIRE. Text obtained by L. C. Wimberly
about 1916 from M. Boynton, Missouri Valley, Iowa.

63. THE FATAL WÉDDING. Text obtained from Blanche Pope of
Red Cloud, Nebraska, about 1914. Still popular in many regions.

64. JESSE JAMES. Text known to Professor Reed Smith (1920)
of the University of South Carolina, as current in that region. The
second text is from Iowa, and was secured by L. C. Wimberly of the
University of Nebraska in 1916. A local ballad which is an adaptation of *Jesse James* is *The Assassinatioh of J. B. Marcum*, printed by
William Aspinwall Bradley in "Song-Ballets and Devil's Ditties,"
Harper's Magazine, May, 1915, p. 901. The origin of *Jesse James*
is unknown. It is possible that it is itself an adaptation.

65. (A) CHARLES GUITEAU. Text secured by Professor E. F.
Piper of the University of Iowa, from a student who had it from
South Dakota. The origin of this song is unknown. Dr. Carl
Van Doren says that he often heard it in Illinois during the 90's
from his father.

(B) THE DEATH OF YOUNG BENDALL. Text from Miss Agnes
Andrews of Cambridge, Nebraska. 1918. She writes of the piece
as follows: "A young man by the name of Bendall whose parents
were supposed to be living in England in wealth came to Canada
about the year 1890 and settled near St. Thomas, Ontario. He soon
made friends with a young married man by the name of J. J. Bircnell.
Birchell, knowing that Bendall carried much gold on his person,
enticed him out on a hunting expedition and very coolly shot him.
The lines of *Young Bendall* were composed and set to music by a
young school teacher in the neighborhood where the tragedy took
place."

A third piece of the same pattern is *John T. Williams*. A
fragment of it from Mrs. E. N. Hardin (1916) of Missouri Valley,
Iowa, who had it from a ranchman at Cambridge, Nebraska, who
had it from Canada, begins as follows:

> My name it is John T. Williams,
> My name I'll never deny,
> I'll leave my dear old parents
> To suffer and to die,
> For murdering . . . .
> Upon the scaffold high.

Their testimony is to the effect that it was sung in the seventies
before the death of Garfield (1881). Other pieces from the same

singers are old, or are closer to their Old World originals than many American texts, so that it is possible that *John T. Williams*, or some other predecessor of *Charles Guiteau* and *Young Bendall*, was the model for these pieces. The song is of a staple pattern and, in its original form, might belong either to the Old or the New World.

66. SAM BASS. Text from Lomax's *Cowboy Songs*, p. 149. N. H. Thorpe, *Songs of the Cowboys* (p. 135), credits the authorship to John Denton, Gainesville, Texas, 1879.

67. JACK WILLIAMS. From a manuscript book of ballads in the possession of L. C. Wimberly, 1916. Probably of British importation. In another Nebraska text, the place names are changed to "Bowery Street" and "Sing Sing."

68. YOUNG MCFEE. Text secured by L. C. Wimberly from Mrs. E. N. Hardin of Missouri Valley, Iowa, 1916. Professor A. H. Tolman prints a much longer text in *The Journal of American Folk-Lore*, vol. 29, p. 186, with the following comment: "This text was obtained through Mrs. Pearl H. Bartholomew from Mrs. M. M. Soners, both of Warren, Indiana. The mother of Mrs. Soners sang it to her almost fifty years ago in Ohio. Mrs. Soners states that the poem records an actual occurrence and that her mother knew Hettie Stout well." Like *The Death of Garfield*, this may be an indigenous ballad, or merely an American adaptation of some older piece. Note the "ten thousand pounds" of the last stanza.

69. BONNY BLACK BESS. Text from Mrs. John Leslie of Stanford, Montana, secured by Mabel Conrad Sullivan of Winnett, Montana, in 1915. A song having the same title and the same hero, but otherwise not identical, appears in Lomax's *Cowboy Songs*, p. 194.

70. TURPIN AND THE LAWYER. A Nova Scotia text. See W. R. Mackenzie, *The Quest of the Ballad* (1919), p. 144. Fragments of the same song, brought from New York, are known in Nebraska.

71. JACK DONAHOO. Text from Lomax's *Cowboy Songs*, p. 64, Practically the same text appears in Nova Scotia. See Mackenzie. *The Quest of the Ballad*, p. 66.

72. CAPTAIN KIDD. Text from *Pilgrims of the Plains* (1913) by Mrs. Kate A. Aplington of Council Groves, Kansas, p. 56. This book contains a number of old songs. Fragments of *Captain Kidd* are still current in scattered places.

73. TEXAS RANGERS. Text obtained from Mrs. Eliza Shelman of Hansen's Ferry, Washington, in 1908. It was learned by her in Nodaway County, Missouri, in her childhood.

74. THE LITTLE OLD SOD SHANTY ON MY CLAIM. Text obtained from Lillian Gear Boswell of Wheatland, Wyoming, 1914. This is an adaptation of the popular negro or psuedo-negro song "The Little Old Log Cabin in the Lane," by Will S. Hays. According to A. J. Leach, the historian of Antelope County, Nebraska, the words were

printed on the backs of cards with the instructions that they were to be sung to the melody of "The Little Old Log Cabin." On the front of the cards were pictures of a sod shanty. See *Modern Language Notes*, January, 1918. Mr. F. W. Schaupp of Lincoln, Nebraska, says that the adaptation was made by a Nebraskan of his acquaintance, Emery Miller, when he was holding down a Nebraska claim in the eighties. Most texts of the song come from the Central Western region. It still has no little currency.

75. COWBOY SONG. Obtained by Frances Francis of Cheyenne from Winthrop Condict of Saratoga, Wyoming, in 1911. It is built upon the religious song, *In the Sweet By and By*. Mr. Lomax prints a slightly different text, *The Cowboy's Dream* in *Cowboy Songs*, p. 18. N. H. Thorpe, *Songs of the Cowboys* (p. 40) ascribes the authorship to the "father of Captain Roberts, of the Texas Rangers." His copy was given to him by Wait Rogers in 1898.

76. THE OLD CHISHOLM TRAIL. Text from Lomax's *Cowboy Songs*, p. 58. See also Thorpe, *Songs of the Cowboys*, p. 109.

77. THE DYING COWBOY. Text secured by Lillian Gear Boswell of Wheatland, Wyoming, in 1914. Brought from Illinois to Wyoming. This is an adaptation of an Irish song, *The Unfortunate Rake*, dating from the eighteenth century. The traces of a military funeral remaining in the chorus of some texts are somewhat incongruous in a cowboy song. For the history of the song see Phillips Barry, *Journal of American Folk-Lore*, vol. 24, p. 341. *The Dying Cowboy* is widely current in the Western states. Adaptation credited by N. H. Thorpe, *Songs of the Cowboys* (p. 41), to Troy Hale, Battle Creek, Nevada.

78. BURY ME NOT ON THE LONE PRAIRIE. Also known as *The Dying Cowboy*. Text obtained by Mabel Conrad Sullivan from Mrs. John Leslie of Stanford, Montana, in 1915. An adaptation of the once popular song *Ocean Burial*, words by W. H. Saunders, music by G. N. Allen. Credited by N. H. Thorpe, *Songs of the Cowboys* (p. 62), to H. Clemons, Deadwood, Dakota, 1872.

79. I WANT TO BE A COWBOY. Text secured by Frances Francis of Cheyenne as sung in Wyoming about 1885. It is an adaptation of the religious song *I Want to Be an Angel*.

80. WHOOPEE TI YI YO, GIT ALONG LITTLE DOGIES. Text from J. A. Lomax's *Cowboy's Songs*, p. 87.

81. CHEYENNE BOYS. Text as sung by Mrs. Jeanetta Gear of Junction, Wyoming, in 1914. This piece is widely current, with various local adaptations. Compare *Mississippi Girls*, Lomax, *Cowboy Songs*, p. 108, *Arizona Boys and Girls*, Thorpe, *Songs of the Cowboys*, p. 1.

82. BREAKING IN A TENDERFOOT. Text obtained from Frances Francis of Cheyenne in 1911. Thought by her to have been locally

composed near Cheyenne. Compare *The Horse Wrangler*, Lomax, p. 136. N. H. Thorpe (p. 146) says the author was Yank Hitson, Denver, Colorado, 1889.

83. STARVING TO DEATH ON A GOVERNMENT CLAIM. Text obtained by Vivian Cleaver Cleveland at Hot Springs, South Dakota, in 1914. Compare *Greer County*, Lomax, p. 278.

84. THE BUFFALO SKINNERS. Text from Lomax's *Cowboy Songs*, p. 158.

85. KINKAIDER'S SONG. Text obtained from Miss Harriet Cook, of Gem, Nebraska, in 1915. A homesteader's song popular in the Nebraska sandhill regions. Sung at picnics, reunions, and the like to the tune of *My Maryland*. Moses P. Kinkaid was congressman of the Sixth Congressional District, 1903–1919. He was the introducer of a bill for 640-acre homesteads known as the "Kinkaid Homestead Law."

86. DAKOTA LAND. Text obtained from Lillian Gear Boswell of Wheatland, Wyoming, in 1914. This piece has for its model and is sung to the melody of the religious song *Beulah Land*.

87. THE DREARY BLACK HILLS. Text obtained from Harry Gear of Junction, Wyoming, in 1914.

88. JOE BOWERS. This version was obtained in 1915 from Mr. Francis Withee of Stella, Nebraska, who heard it sung many times when a freighter in 1862–65 on the Denver-Nebraska City trail. It was a freighter's favorite. The song is supposed to be sung by a Missourian in California about 1849–51. It was in existence as early as 1854.

89. IN THE SUMMER OF SIXTY. Text obtained from Frances Francis of Cheyenne, Wyoming, in 1911.

90. THE DYING CALIFORNIAN. Version secured by L. C. Wimberly as written in a manuscript book from Iowa in 1856. This song has wide currency, usually in somewhat shortened form. It is known also as "The Dying Brother's Farewell," "The Dying Brother's Request," and "The Brother's Request."

91. THE PRETTY MOHEA. Obtained by Mabel Conrad Sullivan from Mrs. John Leslie of Stanford, Montana, 1914. In many texts of this song the name "Mohea" passes into "Maumee," "The Pretty Maumee."

92. (A) KATIE'S SECRET. Text as sung by Mrs. Mary F. Lindsay of Hebron, Nebraska, 1914.

(B) THE HAWTHORN TREE. Text obtained by L. C. Wimberly from a Louisiana source.

93. MARY AND WILLIE. Text obtained by Mabel Conrad Sullivan from Mrs. John Leslie of Stanford, Montana, 1914. This piece seems to be the *Annie and Willie* known, according to Professor Shearin, in the Cumberland Mountains. The plot resembles that of *The Prentice*

Boy (No. 31) and *The Rich Young Farmer* (No. 29). It may also be compared with that of *The Bailiff's Daughter of Islington* (Child, No. 105.)

94. KITTY WELLS. Text secured by Professor Reed Smith in 1920 from a student at the University of South Carolina, J. B. Belk. Mr. Belk had it from his grandmother who heard it sung by slaves in Union County, South Carolina. A version sung by Mrs. Mary F. Lindsay of Hebron, Nebraska, is nearly identical but has an additional stanza.

95. PASTORAL ELEGY. Text obtained by Professor Edwin F. Piper, from a manuscript book belonging to Mrs. Lydia Hinshaw of Richland, Iowa. Mrs. Hinshaw says that it was sung by her mother who knew it when she came to Iowa from Ohio in 1840. "Coroden" is obviously from Corydon.

96. THE COURTSHIP OF BILLY GRIMES. Text of A. J. Leach of Oakdale, Antelope County, Nebraska, in 1914, who learned it as "sung before 1850 in Michigan."

97. FAIR FANNY MOORE. Text obtained from Mrs. John Leslie of Stanford, Montana, 1915. Mr. Lomax's Texas text is nearly identical and the ballad is listed by H. M. Belden as known in Missouri. It still has wide currency.

98. I WISH I WAS SINGLE AGAIN. Text obtained from Lillian Gear Boswell when living at Junction, Wyoming, in 1914. According to H. M. Belden, the authorship of this popular piece is claimed by George Meeks, a ballad singer in Kansas. "A Study in Contemporary Balladry," *The Mid-West Quarterly*, vol. I, p. 170. 1913–14.

99. I'LL NOT MARRY AT ALL. Text obtained from Mabel Conrad Sullivan of Winnett, Montana, 1915.

100. ROSEN THE BOW. Text obtained through Mabel Conrad Sullivan from Mrs. John Leslie of Stanford, Montana, 1915. Other texts, as that of J. A. Lomax in *Cowboy Songs*, spell the title *Rosin the Beau*. The song is printed as an "Old English Song" in *The Franklin Square Song Collection*, No. 2, p. 48 (1884) under the name *Rosin the Bow*, which is probably the original spelling.

101. EVALINA. Text from Marie Gladys Hayden of Hobson, Montana, 1914.

102. MY BLUE-EYED BOY. From a manuscript book of songs from oral transcription in the possession of Sadie Thurman Hewitt of Brokenbow, Nebraska. Transcribed under the date of February, 1905.

103. THE OLD GRAY MULE. Text obtained from Iowa sources by L. C. Wimberly of the University of Nebraska, 1917.

104. (A) I WILL TELL YOU OF A FELLOW. Text obtained from Northeastern Iowa by L. A. Quivey in 1914. The song is usually known as "Common Will." For other versions, see Broadwood and

Maitland, *English County Songs*, p. 52, 1893, and *The Journal of American Folk-Lore*, vol. 28, 173, vol. 29, 171, etc.

105. THE PREACHER'S LEGACY. From Mrs. Hinshaw's manuscript book, had by her from the singing of N. C. Johnson. Her copy is to be dated about 1879. Secured through E. F. Piper.

106. THE SPANISH CABINEER. Text as sung on a ranch at Junction, Wyoming, 1913. Secured by Lillian Gear Boswell. This version of the well-known college song *The Spanish Cavalier* is included because of the interest of the folk-etymological changes of the first stanza.

107. THE TWO DRUMMERS. Text obtained from Mrs. E. N. Hardin, of Missouri Valley, Iowa, in 1916, through L. C. Wimberly. Of interest is the rapid action of its last part. The song is of comparatively recent composition. It is by Edward B. Marks and was published by Joseph Western in 1896. As with *After the Ball, Two Little Girls in Blue*, and other song hits of the 1890's which still have vitality in out of the way places, all knowledge of its authorship and origin is lacking to its singers.

108. THE QUAKER'S COURTSHIP. Text obtained from Iowa by L. C. Wimberly, in 1916. For this song, see Newell, *Games and Songs of American Children* (1903), p. 94. It is an importation from England, like most of the following pieces.

109. DUTCHMAN, DUTCHMAN, WON'T YOU MARRY ME? Text of Miss Edith Little, Falls City, Nebraska, in 1914. This is a variant of the well-known "Soldier, Soldier, Won't You Marry Me?" See Newell, *Games and Songs*, p. 93.

110. WHAT WILL YOU GIVE ME IF I GET UP? Text of Miss Lucia Saxer of Mount Clare, Nebraska, 1914. This song is usually entitled LAZY MARY. It is sometimes used in a singing game. See Newell, *Games and Songs*, p. 96.

111. PAPER OF PINS. Text secured from Louisiana by L. C. Wimberly, in 1916. Compare Newell, *Games and Songs*, p. 52.

112. (A) THE MILKMAID. Text secured from the singing of children at Omaha by Elizabeth Gordon, 1915.

(B) THE PRETTY MILKMAID. Text secured by Frances Botkin and Zora Schaupp from Mrs. Adna Dobson of Lincoln, Nebraska.

113. BILLY BOY. From the singing of Mrs. Ava Shellenbarger of Pawnee City, Nebraska, 1911. This favorite song is an Old World importation. See *The Journal of American Folk-Lore*, vol. 26, p. 357.

114. POOR ROBIN. Text obtained from Nuckolls County, Nebraska, by Miss Alice Hanthorne, in 1915. Other versions have the titles "Old Rover," "Poor Roger," "Poor Johnny," etc. This is an old song. Compare *The Journal of American Folk-Lore*, vol. 13, p. 230, 1900. It is now mostly a motion song in children's games

Compare also Alice Gomme, *Dictionary of British Folk-Lore,* vol. II, p. 16, 1898.

115. BABES IN THE WOODS. Text from Harry Gear of Junction, Wyoming, 1913. This favorite song is still sung by grown-ups in the Kentucky mountains. Compare Bishop Percy's account of the *Children in the Woods, Reliques of Ancient English Poetry* (1865).

116. IN GOOD OLD COLONY TIMES. Text from Mrs. Mary F. Lindsay of Hebron, Nebraska, in 1915. For the history of this song, see *The Ballad of the Three* in A. H. Tolman's "Some Songs Traditional in the United States," *Journal of American Folk-Lore,* vol. 29, p. 167 (1916) and G. L. Kittredge's annotation.

117. LET'S GO TO THE WOODS. Text of Mrs. Mary F. Lindsay. Hebron, Nebraska, 1916. Sometimes known as *Robbin, Bobbin, Richard, and John,* or *The Wren Shooting.* For this song, see the account of St. Stephen's Day customs in G. F. Northall's *English Folk-Rhymes,* 1892. It was printed as a nursery song in *Gammer Gurton's Garland,* 1783.

118. I BOUGHT ME A WIFE. Text obtained by Elizabeth Gordon from Esther Knapp in Omaha, 1915. Miss Knapp's mother learned it in childhood from the singing of another child. For the final couplet, compare a song in a comedy by W. Wager (about 1568), which runs—

> I laid my bridle upon the shelf;
> If you will anymore, sing it yourself.

119. WE'LL ALL GO DOWN TO ROWSER'S. Text from E. R. Harlan of Des Moines, Iowa, 1914. This piece is sometimes merely sung but usually it is a game song.

120. SWEET FIELDS OF VIOLO. Obtained by Mabel Conrad Sullivan from Fern Sikes of Crete, Nebraska, in 1915. The singer should "end the piece with a good crow." This song has some relation to the college or glee club song, *My Father Has Some Very Fine Ducks.*

INDEX

256